"The Survival Guide does a great job of providing business owners with a basic, easy-to-read understanding of qualified retirement plans, how to set them up, how to operate them, and how to get expert help with them."

Michael Canan, *Esq., Author, Qualified Retirement & Other Employee Benefit Plans*

"I enjoyed reading the book, and I believe that you are filling a real information void for business owners interested in providing retirement benefits for employees and themselves. As a professional, I will use this book when working with business owners to communicate more effectively. Congratulations on your work!"

Jim Suellentrop, *Certified Investment Management Consultant*

"The book covers everything you need to know about retirement plans in an easy-to-read and understandable manner. This would be excellent reading for any business owner who has a retirement plan or is contemplating starting one."

Gregory D. Sullivan, *CPA/PFS, CFP, 1995 - 96 Pres., International Assn. for Financial Planning*

"I found this to be a very complete, yet relatively brief exposition of the laws and regulations on a most complex and confusing subject. Nice job."

Bill Mullen, *J.D., CAE, Executive Director, Institute of Investment Management Consultants*

To Lew

I can only aspire to be the writer you are

Dave Cukol

Retirement Plan Survival Guide

Table of Contents

This survival guide offers business owners valuable information about the implementation and operation of retirement plans for themselves and their employees. In order to help you understand this highly technical subject, we have translated the technical expressions used in connection with retirement plans into words anyone who has ever driven a car or taken a journey can understand. Here's a brief overview of the survival guide's contents. A more detailed table of contents can be found at the beginning of each part.

The biggest question in every business owner's mind is "Why should I have a retirement plan?" One main reason is that a "qualified" retirement plan helps you to accumulate funds for retirement by providing significant income tax savings. The tax savings information is highlighted in this part of the survival guide. We also explain some of the rules which must be followed in order to have a qualified retirement plan.

This part of the survival guide discusses the various types of plans available. You should read this part if:

- You don't have a plan and want to get information on the possibilities for your company;

- You have a plan and are not sure if it's the right kind of plan for your business.

Part III. The Owner, the Drivers, and the Mechanics

Many business owners feel that their retirement plans are huge burdens and too much extra work. You should read this part of the survival guide to discover:

- What roles need to be filled to operate a plan;
- What professionals are available to help with plan management;
- Where to turn when you know you need help;
- What you should expect from your team.

Part IV. The Rules of the Road

In exchange for the tax advantages that come with a qualified retirement plan, there are a host of rules which must be followed. This part of the survival guide highlights what the government expects from you as a retirement plan fiduciary and who will enforce the rules. It explains:

- All of the rules you must meet;
- How you and your plan must conform to the rules;
- What can happen to you if you don't comply with the rules.

Part V. On the Road

The core of any retirement plan is the investments used, their performance, and their ultimate distribution to participants in the form of benefits. This part of the survival guide addresses:

- Components of a good investment policy statement;
- Who should direct the plan's investments;
- Investment selection criteria;
- What investments you can't make in a retirement plan.

To keep the plan running smoothly, and in order to stay in compliance with Internal Revenue Service and Department of Labor rules, accurate records should be kept and investment performance tracked regularly. This part of the survival guide addresses:

- Plan record keeping;
- Tracking investment performance;
- Participants' rights;
- Processing distributions;
- Retirement benefits in divorce cases;
- Benefit claims and appeals.

It's important to understand your options with your retirement plan funds at retirement. This part of the survival guide helps you understand:

- Age restrictions on access to funds;
- Whether to make a tax-free IRA rollover or take the money and pay the taxes;
- Hidden taxes;
- Beneficiary designations.

Introduction

Have you ever been on a car trip and realized along the way that you didn't have accurate directions, a map, or even someone to ask for help? As a result, did you find yourself on the wrong route? Did you start out thinking you would reach your destination rather effortlessly, but found out on the road that you overlooked the potential obstacles of the trip?

Like an ill-fated car trip, many business owners naively embark upon the journey of establishing a company retirement plan with the aim of easily accumulating funds for themselves and their employees. Unfortunately, barriers such as complex pension laws, administrative details, lack of financial knowledge, and poor investment decisions may cause the plan to become more of a liability than an asset to their company.

The rules for operating a retirement plan can be cumbersome and confusing. This is particularly aggravating to busy owners who already have enough details to handle in running their own businesses. Although there are many technical and comprehensive guides to understanding plan management, there are few, if any, practical, easy-to-understand guides on creating and maintaining a plan as a business owner.

As advisors to retirement plan fiduciaries (usually the business owners themselves), we determined that there needed to be not only an "owner's manual" for the retirement vehicle, but a "road map" for the journey. Therefore, we have produced this *Business Owner's Retirement Plan Survival Guide*. To make matters easier, this guide will translate many of the technical expressions used by plan administrators, attorneys, CPAs, and investment advisors into words anyone who has ever driven a car or taken a journey can understand.

You should bear in mind that this guide is a general summary only; it doesn't cover all aspects of the laws that are summarized or all of the laws that affect retirement plans. It shouldn't be construed as specific legal or investment advice. If specific advice is desired or if you want more information, you should consult with a qualified advisor who is well versed in these issues.

Part I.

Why Go on the Retirement Plan Trip?

The contents of this part of the survival guide are:

One of the greatest challenges of any individual's life is how to be financially secure at retirement. Statistically, it's said that only 5 percent achieve that goal. The remaining 95 percent must keep working, rely on others, or greatly reduce their standard of living.

A. The Benefits of Using a "Qualified" Retirement Plan

Setting up a retirement savings program that fosters consistent annual contributions and investment growth is the key to achieving your goal of financial independence. The big question is "Why save in a 'qualified' retirement plan?" The three big reasons are that every dollar saved in a "qualified plan" (that is, one which satisfies the tax rules for qualification):

- Is tax deductible for the year for which it is made;
- Grows without taxes every year until withdrawal; and
- Is not taxable until funds are received.

This is a powerful combination that helps your retirement savings grow rapidly! Another option, of course, is to build your retirement nest egg without a formalized plan, simply opting to place those funds in the investments of choice. Keep in mind that in this case taxes are paid every year and they will take a substantial and highly avoidable bite out of your earnings.

Compare the figures when savings are outside a plan versus inside a plan.[1]

	Without a Plan	With a Plan
Cash available	$10,000	$10,000
Less taxes at 31% tax bracket	(3,100)	-0-
Balance left to invest	6,900	10,000
8% interest earned	552	800
Less taxes due	171	-0-
Net interest earned	381	800
Plus amount invested	6,900	10,000
Amount at end of year	$7,281	$10,800
Difference in one year (before tax on distribution)		**+$3,519**

Number of Years	Without a Plan	With a Plan	Difference
10	$94,000	$156,000	+$62,000
20	254,000	494,000	+240,000
30	529,000	1,223,000	+694,000

[1]Assumptions used for next three calculations: 1. The amount of cash available per year is $10,000 before income taxes. 2. Investments earn 8 percent yearly. 3. You are in the 31 percent tax bracket.

Don't you still have to pay taxes when the plan assets are distributed? You bet. But the advantages are still quite formidable. As the following table illustrates, the earlier you start, the better shape you're in.[1]

Number of Years	Without a Plan After Tax	With a Plan[1] After Tax	Difference After Tax
10	$94,000	$119,000	+$25,000
20	254,000	328,000	+74,000
30	529,000	768,000	+239,000

Even after paying tax on the plan distributions, there are advantages!

- You have more retirement dollars with a plan.
- Qualified plan assets are protected from creditors.
- The savings are consistent since plans are usually funded yearly—personal savings tends to be hit or miss.
- Your tax bracket may be lower in the future at retirement than today when you are employed.

These illustrations show you how saving for your financial independence goal is greatly enhanced by investing current tax savings and having a structure that supports yearly additions. It's no wonder that retirement plans are one of the fastest-growing segments in the investment industry.

Please note: A business owner must always weigh the financial benefit he or she gets vs. the cost to the owner of covering the employees and complying with the various qualification rules, discussed below. A third party administrator or other consultant can project these figures based on different plan designs so an owner can make a proper decision.

B. The Special Rules for "Qualified" Retirement Plans

As explained above, there are important tax advantages to saving in a "qualified" retirement plan. However, in order for a retirement plan to be "qualified" it must meet a number of additional tax rules which do not apply to nonqualified retirement plans.

Here's a brief summary of the major tax qualification rules for retirement plans:

- The Plan Formality Requirement—This rule requires that a qualified retirement plan be set forth in a written document which con-

---

[1]Assumes a lump sum distribution after age 59½ using 1996 married federal tax rates. Usually people don't withdraw all money at retirement. They take it out over the retirement lifetime, reducing this tax calculation. Instead of the top tax bracket used for calculation, such as 39.6 percent in this example, someone may not pay more than the 28 percent top federal tax bracket when money is withdrawn over a number of years.

tains many of the plan qualification rules (discussed below) as well as a number of definitions and operational provisions which are designed to protect participants and ensure that the plan will be operated in accordance with the Employee Retirement Income Security Act of 1974 (ERISA).

- Coverage and Participation Rules—These rules require that each qualified retirement plan cover a certain number or percentage of a company's lower-paid employees. These rules also specify how long you can "hold out" employees from participating in the company plan. One of these rules establishes a minimum size for each retirement plan maintained by a company (or group of related companies). The rule is designed to prevent a company from maintaining a "special" retirement plan which covers only the owner of the company while all of the other eligible employees are covered under a "comparable" plan.

- Nondiscrimination Rules—These rules are designed to prevent discrimination in benefits, contributions, or the availability of plan features (e.g., the right to obtain participant loans) which favors the highly paid employees. The nondiscrimination rules do *not* prevent a company from discriminating against highly paid employees. There are special nondiscrimination rules and tests applicable to 401(k) plans.

- Vesting Rules[1]—These rules specify the maximum acceptable periods for "vesting" a participant's benefit under a plan. While there are several acceptable vesting schedules which can be used to determine when a participant's benefit becomes nonforfeitable, companies are free to adopt more favorable vesting schedules.

- Distribution Rules—There are a number of interrelated rules concerning distributions from qualified retirement plans. These rules govern when a participant can receive a distribution from a retirement plan, what notices and elections must be given to a participant before a participant can actually receive his money, and the various methods for making a distribution. These rules also cover the earliest time a distribution can be made as well as the latest time a participant can defer the receipt of benefits from a plan.

- Top-Heavy Rules—These rules apply only to small- and medium-sized plans which primarily benefit the owners of the business or "key" employees. If a plan is determined to be a "top-heavy" plan (i.e., relatively more money has been set aside for higher paid employees), then special (more restrictive) vesting and contribution rules will apply.

- Section 415 Limits on Benefits—Internal Revenue Code section 415 places a limit on how much can be set aside in either a defined contribution plan or a defined benefit plan for each participant.

---

[1]Vesting means the schedule by which an employee earns a nonforfeitable interest in his retirement benefit.

There is a separate limit for amounts allocated each year to a participant's account under a defined contribution plan and a separate limit for the amount of benefits which can be paid out each year for an individual retiring under a defined benefit plan. There is also a combined limit, in effect through 1999, that applies to individuals who are participating (or who in the past may have participated) in both a defined contribution plan and a defined benefit plan.

This is only a brief summary of the various qualification rules which will apply to your business' retirement plan. Because of the constantly changing complexity of these rules, we strongly recommend that you seek the advice of qualified advisors (see Part III of this survival guide) in order to help you meet these various requirements.

Part II.
Getting Ready for the Trip

The contents of this part of the survival guide are:

"This baby will get you 90 grand a year
. . . starting at age 55!"

A. The Importance of Choosing the Right Retirement Vehicle

The process of accumulating sufficient retirement savings might be likened to traveling up a mountain. There are many ways to get up a mountain—straight up a steep grade, gradually up a winding road, or slowly curving around the mountain. Some mountains (retirement goals) are higher than others. There are different vehicles you can use to travel up a mountain. There is also a wide variety of retirement plans from which you can choose. The tricky part is finding the one that best suits your needs.

Before you begin your trip up the mountain, you need to pick the best available vehicle for your route. You'll need the right amount of horsepower to negotiate the steeper slopes along the way. Can you afford a car with a little bit of extra "umph"? If so, you might be better able to pass unexpected obstacles like that fully loaded 18-wheeler crawling up the grade ahead of you. Conversely, selection of the correct retirement plan (or combination of plans) can ensure that you and your employees will reach your personal summit (or financial goal) by retirement in a timely, cost-effective manner.

B. Important Considerations

Let's begin with an overall picture of where you are in the retirement planning process. First of all, you, the employer, are a certain age and can predict a certain income level, with or without some degree of fluctuation, based on the performance of the company. Now come the long-range decisions that frequently get lost in the shuffle of day-to-day life.

1. When Do You Want to Retire?

Big Question Number One: When do you want to retire? Have you thought about that one yet? It might still be many years away, but if you start planning now, your long-range financial objectives will be a lot easier to achieve.

2. How Much Income Will You Need?

Big Question Number Two: How much income will you need at the time of retirement to maintain your desired standard of living for the rest of your days? The answer, of course, varies with individual circumstances and desires. Life in a mobile home next to a lake full of trout is obviously a great deal less expensive than world travel and five-star restaurants. Which sounds better to you? Perhaps something in the middle.

In any event, the better you understand the retirement lifestyle you'd like to live, the easier it'll be to plan a strategy to get you there. A qualified professional can take a comprehensive look at your current financial situation, including the value of your business and other sources of income, add your objectives to the equation, and come up with a fairly accurate estimate of the future income level you will need.

That's a good idea, and we urge you to do that. For the time being, however, you can work with the rule of thumb that you will need approximately 70 percent to 80 percent of your preretirement income to maintain your current lifestyle.

In other words, if you were planning to retire this year and now earn $50,000, you may need between $35,000 and $40,000 per year to meet your needs. The reason you'll probably need less money is quite simple. Most people, by the time they draw their

careers to a close, have either paid or substantially paid their mortgages, the kids are out of college and on their own, and their income tax brackets are lower. Thus, they generally have lower expenses. While this might or might not be the case for you, it helps to underscore the necessity of good planning.

3. Should Your Company Offer a Retirement Plan?

Big Question Number Three: Should your company offer a retirement plan? Consider the following:

- How much you and your company can afford to contribute to a retirement plan;
- Whether your company can make its contributions on a regular basis, year after year;
- Whether you are interested in providing retirement benefits to all employees, or just to a select group of employees;
- The rate at which you accumulate investment earnings or investment growth within your retirement plan; and
- Your willingness and ability to follow the "rules of the road" which apply to qualified retirement plans.[1]

Each employee's current age can be viewed as the starting point of their climb up the mountain, with a projected arrival of, let's say, age 65. They'll need to accumulate a given amount of money by that time, with resources that have already been accumulated and additional money that will be generated between now and then. The major variables include how much time each individual has remaining in the work force, how much money the company will contribute, how much money the employee will contribute (if the plan allows), the investment growth of those funds on a tax-deferred basis, and the amount of money that can be saved outside of the retirement plan.

C. Types of Plans Available

The retirement plans described below are essentially vehicles designed to get you from where you are now to your objective of a comfortable retirement. Since the term "comfortable" means different things to different people, it might be better to view your company's retirement plan as a group of separate vehicles offering your employees various options so that everyone can reach their preferred retirement lifestyle.

That's not to say they'll be able to back up the moving van to the Taj Mahal (if they can, we'd like to talk to them), but a viable retirement plan needs to do different things for different people. A long-

---

[1] If you are not willing to provide some benefits to your rank and file employees, a qualified plan may not be the right approach for you. You might consider the pros and cons of a nonqualified deferred compensation plan with your tax advisor.

term strategy best suited to younger employees might be economically disastrous to senior members of your team who are closer to retirement. Conversely, a plan with accelerated accumulations just prior to retirement might be completely useless to a 23-year-old administrative assistant, particularly if that employee leaves within a few years.

While the list of options for retirement plans is quite extensive, most fall into two basic categories: **Defined Benefit Plans** and **Defined Contribution Plans.** In a nutshell, the difference breaks down to whether employees will know how much they'll be getting upon retirement, or whether everyone will have to take an educated spin at the investment game and see what comes out the other side.

1. Defined Benefit Plans

In general, under a defined benefit plan, the benefit is defined so that the employees know the amount of the benefit that they will receive at retirement. These plans usually pay a specific monthly amount beginning at retirement and continuing for the remainder of the employee's life (and possibly the life of a surviving spouse). In many cases, the amount is calculated as a percentage of the employee's average compensation.

For example, Nick's Body Shop's sole shareholder, Nick Fender, would like to provide the maximum retirement benefit for himself (he's age 55) and he's willing to provide a similar benefit for his younger employees. The corporation adopts a defined benefit plan that calls for a lifetime benefit, commencing at age 65, equal to 4 percent of the participant's average compensation times years of service up to 25 years. If Nick's average compensation is $100,000 and he works for 25 years, the plan will pay him a benefit of $100,000 per year for life.

Defined benefit plans do not maintain an individual account for each participant. Instead, the assets are pooled together and the company makes an agreement that the plan will pay a defined benefit to each employee. Since the rules for these plans make the company responsible for contributing enough funds to the plan to pay the promised benefits, the company bears the risks (and rewards) of the plan's investment experience. Thus, if the plan's investment returns are significantly less than expected, the company may be required to dig deeper into its own pockets to make up for the shortfall.

In order to keep things on the right track, you'll need the services of an actuary. The actuary's job is to make economic projections to determine how much money will be required each year to provide the promised benefits upon retirement. This person grapples with interest rate assumptions as well as other assumptions about the plan and its participants. Working with figures based on

the number of employees and their respective ages, an actuary can determine the necessary contributions with reasonable accuracy.

In some respects, the defined benefit plan is somewhat like a bus which is being driven by a "bus driver," the actuary. Here, each participant can basically sit back knowing that if he remains with the company, he will receive the promised retirement benefits down the road.

Many middle-sized and larger institutions prefer this type of plan because it's easy for participants to understand what they will get and when they will get it. On the other hand, defined benefit plans typically favor long-term and older employees and may not provide any significant advantage to those who leave the company early in their careers. Businesses with many younger employees or frequent employee turnover often find that a defined benefit plan is not viewed as a meaningful benefit by their employees. But this type of plan can encourage employee longevity.

2. Defined Contribution Plans

Defined contribution plans do not provide a specific level or amount of money upon retirement. Instead, the amount to be contributed to each participant's account under the plan each year is defined (by either a fixed formula or by giving the employer the discretion to decide how much to contribute each year). The size of a participant's benefit will depend on:

- The amounts of money contributed to the individual's account by the employer and, perhaps, by the employee as well;
- The rate of investment growth on the principal;
- How long the money remains in the plan (in most cases, the employee, upon retirement, has the option of either receiving the payment in a lump sum or by taking partial payments on a regular basis while the balance continues to earn interest); and
- Whether the forfeitures of participants who leave before they are fully vested are shared among the remaining participants as a reward to long-term employees.

Since benefits accumulate on an individual basis, these plans are sometimes referred to as "individual account plans." In these plans, unlike in defined benefit plans, the risk (and reward) of investment experience is borne by the participant. Defined contribution plans can permit, and sometimes require, that employees make contributions to the plan on either a pretax basis (as in a 401(k) plan) or an after-tax basis (as in a thrift plan). They may also, but are not required to, permit employees to decide how the monies contributed into their accounts will be invested.

In many respects, a defined contribution plan is like an automobile carrier truck (this is the plan vehicle) loaded with separate cars (these are the employees' individual accounts). If the plan trustee (the carrier driver) decides to manage all of the plan's investments on a "pooled" basis, then all of the individual accounts (the cars) stay loaded on the carrier and move up the mountain together at the same pace. However, if the plan trustee decides to allow participants to direct the investment of their accounts, as described in Part V, Section B.3, then when each of the separate cars (the individual accounts) is able to reach the mountain top will depend on how their drivers (the participants) manage the investments within their accounts.

There are five major types, or "models,"of defined contribution plans:

a. Profit Sharing Plans

Profit sharing plans accumulate money through company contributions to an account for each eligible employee. The size of the contribution is generally based on the employee's level of compensation. These plans are highly popular these days—and for good reason! A profit sharing plan allows the company to determine (within certain limits) the amount of money to be contributed each year. The obvious advantage is that management is not locked into a potentially destabilizing expense if business is slow or the economy is sour.

In a good year you might want to contribute as much as 15 percent of employee compensation to your profit sharing plan. In a devastating year you might make no contribution at all. If, however, payments are not made on a continuing basis, the IRS might rule that the plan has been terminated, in which case the participants become fully vested.

For example, Mitch L. Linn owns his own tire sales and repair business. He would like to have a retirement plan, but he does not want to be obligated to make a contribution each year in any given amount. A profit sharing plan is a good choice for Mitch. In a good year he can contribute up to 15 percent of the participants' compensation and he need not contribute anything when his bottom line is a big "0."

b. Money Purchase Plans

A money purchase plan is similar to a profit sharing plan, except that the rate of contribution is a fixed percentage for each year, such as 10 percent of each eligible employee's compensation. Although the rate can be amended if necessary, small or newer businesses might be well-advised to avoid these plans until they are confident that they can meet the annual contribution requirement. The advantage to money purchase plans over profit sharing plans is that the income tax deductible contribution is not limited to 15 percent of compensation—it can be as high as 25 percent of compensation. However, these plans are subject to somewhat more cumbersome distribution rules than profit sharing plans.

For example, Mitch has now determined that he has a good, rich business and that he can make a larger contribution to a retirement plan each year. So, in addition to the profit sharing plan, he adopts a money purchase plan that calls for a contribution each year equal to 10 percent of the participants' compensation. Between the two plans, he can contribute between 10 percent and 25 percent of compensation each year.

c. Target Benefit Plans

A target benefit plan is a variation of a money purchase plan, except you might say it looks into the rear-view mirror. Instead of starting with a fixed percentage, these plans specify a given benefit, such as 50 percent of salary at retirement, and base each participant's contribution on the amount of money needed to satisfy that obligation.

The age of the employee plays a significant role here. Older workers, obviously, have a shorter time span to accumulate the necessary funds compared to their younger counterparts. In other words, the contribution for an older employee will be higher than the contribution for a younger employee making the same amount of money. It's also important to be aware that the actual retirement benefit is not guaranteed and will depend largely upon investment earnings of each participant's account.

For example, Mitch, now age 55, has determined that he needs to receive a larger relative share of the company's contributions since he'll retire earlier than his younger staff. So, he adopts a target benefit plan that skews the contributions based upon a combination of the participants' relative age and compensation.

d. Cash or Deferred Arrangements (or 401(k) Plans)

A 401(k) plan, sometimes known as a salary deferral or cash or deferred arrangement, allows each of your eligible employees to specify the amount of pretax income that should be deducted from his pay check and placed into a retirement account on his behalf. Flexibility is key here, in that the participants are able to set the deduction levels that best suit their personal situations.

Unfortunately, some people fail to look very far in advance and, thus, discover a severe problem when retirement is just around the corner. To help counter this unfortunate element of human nature, many companies offer matching contributions to encourage their employees to make salary deferrals. The maximum amount which an employee can contribute is currently limited to $9,500. This amount changes periodically and is published by the Internal Revenue Service.

For example, Mitch decides that his employees should contribute toward their own retirement rather than relying just on the contributions he makes as the business owner. Therefore, he amends the profit sharing plan to add a cash or deferred arrangement to the plan under which each employee can reduce his cash compensation and redirect these amounts to the plan. In order to inspire his employees to participate in the plan out of their own pockets, Mitch will match their contributions with a 50¢ on the dollar basis up to 5 percent of compensation.

e. Stock Bonus Plans and Employee Stock Ownership Plans

Stock bonus plans and employee stock ownership plans (ESOPs) are designed to use your company stock as a mechanism for building equity that will become a retirement resource for your employees.

An ESOP, by meeting certain additional requirements, can even borrow money from a bank, the company, or a selling shareholder in order to purchase company stock. Since your company can contribute stock instead of cash to the plan, it can obtain a "cashless" tax deduction. However, this strategy can become quite complicated because it requires periodic, independent appraisals of your company's stock and may, in difficult times, require you to explain why the value of your company's stock has declined. One objection that business owners may have to an ESOP is that the company's financial information becomes public knowledge.

In many respects, a stock bonus plan, or ESOP, has the attributes of either a profit sharing plan or a money purchase plan depending upon whether the plan has a fixed obligation to repay money which it has borrowed.

An ESOP has an inherent instability, in that the value of the stock at the time of retirement can vary widely from earlier projections. It can fall far short of its mark if the stock fails to perform well. On the other hand, the retiree might sustain a large windfall if the stock "goes through the roof."

Nick Fender is nearing retirement and ready to collect on his defined benefit plan (see above). However, he realizes that he has no one to pass his business to (his daughter, Buffy, has no interest in the business), that his young employees have expressed an interest in acquiring the business, and that their benefits under the defined benefit plan are rather meager. One solution would be for Nick's Body Shop to adopt an ESOP and for Nick to sell his stock to the ESOP using money borrowed from the local bank. Ultimately, the employees own the company.

f. Special Feature to Consider When Designing Defined Contribution Plans

Defined contribution plans can allow participants to direct their own investment accounts. This is a popular option because:

- The trustees' investment decisions are simplified; and
- The fiduciary responsibility of the trustees is reduced—although not completely eliminated.

See Part V, Section B.3 for details.

D. The Exoticar or the Economodel?—Plan Design Considerations

When selecting the best retirement strategy for you and your company, the two primary considerations will be the overall size of the desired retirement benefit as well as your company's financial ability to meet the resulting obligations. Some plans, such as defined benefit plans and 401(k)s, are subject to more rules and are more expensive to maintain.[1] Other plans might provide a reasonable retirement benefit at a lower cost and would, thus, be more appealing. In either event, the main objective is to choose a strategy that the company can afford down the road—or up the road, as our mountain traveler would see it.

If you are a typical business owner, a company retirement plan will make sense to you only if it provides a larger share of the retirement benefits for you and your most important employees relative to the benefits you must provide to your other employees under the law. To a large extent, the ability of a company retirement plan to

---

[1]Some employers who are looking for the benefits of a qualified plan, but without the hassle, might consider adopting a simplified employee pension or "SEP." Although SEPs are much easier to set up and maintain than qualified retirement plans, they lack much of the design flexibility that many business owners are looking for. Starting in 1997, employers also can adopt either a SIMPLE IRA or SIMPLE 401(k) plan.

provide a certain level of benefits to a targeted group (i.e., the owner and key employees) at an acceptable cost (for other employees) will depend on the details of how you design your plan. You might think of this as "customizing" your retirement vehicle.

Just as you have a wide variety of options available when you purchase a new vehicle, you have many choices to make in order to customize your retirement plan. These choices include options such as:

1. **Eligibility requirements**
   - Setting a minimum age requirement, such as age 21
   - Setting a minimum service requirement, such as 1 year
   - Excluding members of certain employee classifications (e.g., collectively bargained employees)

2. **Setting a benefit or contribution level (or formula)**

3. **Deciding whether to consider Social Security contributions in your formula (this is also known as using "integration" or "permitted disparity")**

4. **Choosing a vesting schedule (when benefits become nonforfeitable)**
   - 100 percent immediately
   - 100 percent after five years
   - 20 percent after three years and then 20 percent per year

5. **Selecting methods of distribution**
   - Lump sum only
   - Annuities
   - Installments

6. **Deciding when employees can receive distributions**
   - Immediately upon termination of employment
   - Must wait until age 65

7. **Determining the plan's normal and early retirement ages**

8. **Deciding how forfeitures (these are nonvested benefits of employees who leave) will be handled**
   - Allocated to other participants
   - Reduce employer contributions

9. Deciding whether participant loans are allowed or not

10. Deciding whether participants will be allowed to direct the investment of their accounts or not

This list of options is just a partial list to give an indication of the many choices that must be made. Some options are not available on all models and some options are mandatory. For example, a defined benefit pension plan must offer certain annuity distribution options (the V-12 engine comes only with the six-speed transmission). You should seek the assistance of a qualified retirement professional when working through these options so that you understand what options are available and the significance of choosing one over another.

Note: If you own or are involved in more than one business, the controlled group or affiliated service group rules may prevent you from having a plan for only one of your companies. You should seek the advice of a qualified professional who understands these complex rules in order to determine if and how they affect your situations.

Overestimating the company's ability to maintain and make payments on retirement plans is one of the most expensive employee benefit mistakes faced by management. With proper advice, you should be able to select the right plan, with the right accessories, to keep everything rolling along smoothly. Since you're looking for a strategy that will work well for the long haul, many business owners are well advised to start out with a modest plan (such as a profit sharing plan) and eventually upgrade to a plan which offers greater benefits upon retirement.

ACTION: *If you have a plan, are you in the right type of plan? Contact an employee benefits attorney or a third party administrator to determine if there are other types of plans that would be better for your company.*

If you don't have a plan, contact an employee benefits attorney or a third party administrator for an analysis of which plan, if any, makes sense for your company.

Part III.
The Owner, the Drivers, and the Mechanics

The contents of this part of the survival guide are:

Many people are involved in the direct and indirect operation and maintenance of a vehicle. The same will be true for your retirement plan. In a small business, the business owner may play several roles—more specifically, that of the plan sponsor, the trustee, and the plan administrator. Further details on these responsibilities are coming right up.

The Business Owner Can Have a Court of Advisors:

Or, the Business Owner Can Play Several Roles:

A. The Role of the Employer

The role of the employer (the business owner) is to:

- Design the plan (with the assistance of qualified professionals);
  - Make payments to the plan;
  - Administer the plan or appoint someone else to take care of its day-to-day responsibilities;
  - Act as trustee—or hire one;
  - Appoint a third party administrator;
- Adopt an investment policy; and
- Make executive decisions involving amendment or termination of the plan.

Sounds like a lot, doesn't it? As sponsor of the retirement plan, the employer's job is to make final decisions on the overall strategy, the projected retirement benefits, and the categories of employees who can participate. The employer also decides the general manner in which the plan will be administered, as well as the circumstances under which it will be revised or replaced.

Once the overall objectives have been determined, the employer needs to adopt a retirement plan document and a retirement trust document. These must be in place before the end of the employer's fiscal year if an income tax deduction is desired for that fiscal year.[1] The employer must then select a plan administrator and the trustee(s). He may hire other help such as a third party administrator (or TPA).

The next step is to provide funds for the retirement plan, recognizing that, generally, once the employer contributes funds to the trust, they cannot be taken out by the employer.

Finally, the employer has final authority over how money paid into the fund will be invested, unless the retirement plan is set up to allow the participants to independently direct their own accounts. In most cases, however, day-to-day decisions involving the investments are left to the trustees. More on trustees later.

B. The Role of the Plan Administrator

The role of the plan administrator is to:

- Develop appropriate written policies and procedures for the operation of the plan;
- Advise participants and beneficiaries on how the plan works;
- Assure compliance with laws and plan qualification requirements;
- Keep track of participants' vesting[2] and benefit amounts;
- Make decisions on benefit claims and distribution of benefits; and
- Establish policies and procedures for participants to borrow money from the plan, if borrowing is allowed under the plan.

The plan administrator is responsible for the general operation of the retirement plan. Remember, the administrator might be the employer or perhaps another individual selected by the owner for the job. A third option would be an "administrative committee," made up of key executives familiar with personnel matters who will consider the various issues brought before them and vote on proposed solutions.

---

[1] If an employer doesn't get around to setting up a qualified plan by the employer's fiscal year end, the employer might still be able to obtain a tax deduction for that year by setting up a SEP prior to the employer's tax filing date.

[2] Vesting refers to the percentage of a participant's benefit that the participant will receive when a distribution is made.

The plan administrator's duties include interpreting the plan document to determine who is eligible to participate, based upon the terms of the plan installed by the employer. Such factors might include, for example, a minimum 21 years of age and a full year of service with the company. The plan administrator also maintains the paperwork for both the employer and any interested government agencies, such as the Internal Revenue Service, the Department of Labor, and the Pension Benefit Guaranty Corporation. Most plan administrators find it necessary to obtain help from a third party administrator (description below) to meet these record keeping and reporting requirements.

C. The Role of the Trustees

The role of the trustees is to:

- Administer the investment of plan assets;

- Distribute benefits, based on instructions from the plan administrator; and

- Report to the plan administrator.

The trustees administer the investments of all assets paid into the retirement plan and distribute benefits pursuant to the instructions of the plan administrator (see above). Appointed by the employer at the time that the retirement plan is established, trustees can be individuals, such as company owners or key employees, or institutions, such as a trust company or the trust department of a bank. If there is more than one trustee, they may share responsibility for all duties equally or each might become personally responsible for specific duties. In either case, an accurate understanding of the expectations for each trustee is crucial from the outset.

The trustees receive retirement fund contributions from the employer plus any additional money paid into the plan by the employees. They then invest those assets to faithfully meet the objectives of the plan, within the guidelines of the Employee Retirement Income Security Act (ERISA), of course. Their performance is monitored through regular reports submitted to the plan administrator.

Some defined contribution plans allow participants to direct the investment of their own accounts. For more about this, see Part V, Section B.3. Under such arrangements, the role of the trustees is to execute those instructions in an efficient and timely fashion on behalf of the participants. Contrary to popular belief, however, this feature doesn't absolve the trustees from responsibilities associated with the selection of investment choices or the ongoing monitoring of investment choices.

D. The Role of the Third Party Administrator (TPA)

The role of the TPA is to:

- Advise the employer and the plan administrator;
- Assist the plan administrator with record keeping and reporting;
- Assist the trustees with trust accounting;
- Calculate contribution levels; and
- Track benefit amounts and vesting.

Many employers and plan administrators are either not familiar with the rules and regulations that govern retirement plans or do not have the human resources to handle the administrative requirements in-house. Under these circumstances, they are well advised to hire third party advisors to help out. This so-called "third party administrator" (TPA) will generally work with the employer, the plan administrator, and sometimes even the trustees in determining who meets eligibility requirements, the size of the contributions, and the extent of the participants' benefits. TPAs also assist with various forms of paperwork and in verifying the plan's compliance with the numerous pension laws. This function is extremely important because a plan ruled out of compliance can be disqualified, substantial taxes and fines can be imposed, or both. We recommend that you have a written service agreement with your TPA in order to avoid misunderstandings.

Although a TPA can provide important assistance, all responsibility ultimately falls on the employer and the plan administrator to make sure that the plan is properly maintained. The TPA may give advice, but the employer and plan administrator must make the decisions and oversee the operation of the plan.

E. The Role of the Registered Investment Advisor (RIA)

The role of the RIA is to:

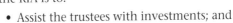

- Assist the trustees with investments; and
- Assist the participants with self-directed accounts.

The registered investment advisor, or RIA, may be appointed by the trustees, the employer, or the plan administrator to assist the trustees in their investment obligations. The RIA is typically responsible for the investment of trust assets, in whole or in part. Since RIAs must meet federal standards, these individuals may absorb substantial responsibility that cannot ordinarily be shifted by the trustees to other fiduciaries. If the plan allows participants to self-direct their accounts, the RIA can play an important role in helping the participants make decisions that could permanently impact their futures.

F. The Role of the Investment Professional

The role of the investment professional is to:

- Recommend the placement of plan assets in various investments.

Although the responsibility for screening, monitoring, and recommending potential investments may be delegated to the insurance agent, stockbroker, or other investment person by the trustees, the liability to the plan still lies with the trustees as to the selection and performance of the investments.

G. The Role of the Actuary

The role of the actuary is to:

- Calculate contribution levels for defined benefit plans and target benefit plans only (not necessary for other types of plans).

The services of an actuary will be needed if your company adopts a defined benefit plan or a target benefit plan. An actuary is a person, trained in mathematics and statistics, who calculates the contributions that must be paid to a defined benefit plan or a target benefit plan in order to fund the promised benefits as they become payable. As you might recall from our earlier description of such plans, participants earn benefits over a specified period of time and the difference in contribution levels among the participants reflects each individual's age, years of service with the company, compensation, and the amount of time remaining before retirement.

H. The Role of the Employee Benefits Attorney

The role of the employee benefits attorney is to:

- Provide legal advice concerning the design and operation of a plan;
- Assist with government audits;
- Guard against prohibited transactions; and
- Assist with the preparation and review of documents.

Retaining the services of a qualified employee benefits attorney can make a vast difference in both the effectiveness of your retirement plan and the ease with which it can be put together. From the beginning, your attorney should be able to provide expert advice on overall strategy and development of the plan itself, plus answer any questions surrounding the roles and responsibilities of all parties involved. Once you are on your way, the attorney should also review plan and trust documents, participant communications, the overall operation of the plan and, most crucially, any audits or investigations by the Internal Revenue Service or Department of Labor. Many of the laws applicable to retirement plans are extremely complex, especially with matters involving loans from the plan, controlled groups and affiliated service groups (as defined in IRS rules), and the divorce of participants. A violation can result in fines, otherwise avoidable excise taxes, and even the disqualification of the entire plan. This is precisely why it's important to work with a competent specialist from the outset.

I. The Role of the Certified Public Accountant (CPA)

The role of the CPA is to:

- Handle trust accounting;
- Prepare and review tax returns and distribution reports; and
- Verify the trust financial reports through a financial audit.

The assistance of a skilled CPA can also make life easier for top level fiduciaries. The CPA will audit the financial statements that go to the Department of Labor. In addition, the CPA should be able to determine whether any of the plan's investments result in unrelated business taxable income, or UBTI. If the trust income includes UBTI, the trustees must file income tax returns and pay resulting income taxes. Thorough familiarity by the CPA with both the government's reporting rules and the UBTI rules will be necessary because problems in these areas can cause substantial penalties.

J. The Role of the Participants

The role of the participants is to:

- Contribute to the plan (if required or if permitted);
- Direct investment of own accounts (if permitted);
- Borrow from the plan (if permitted); and
- Keep up-to-date and informed on plan results.

Generally speaking, the role of the participants is simply to arrive at the point of retirement and receive the benefits accrued. Each participant also has the right to obtain certain information about the plan and his or her benefits, and to receive this information from the plan administrator within a reasonable period of time after the request is made. Participants must also be encouraged to inform the plan administrator of changes in their marital status, mailing address, and intended beneficiaries.

But as we've mentioned earlier, there are ways in which employees can take a hands-on approach, if the retirement plan is established with these opportunities in mind. The participants may choose to make their own contributions under a cash or deferred arrangement—a 401(k) plan—thus helping to build a larger retirement benefit than they would otherwise receive. Another option is to direct their own investments under a defined contribution plan that permits self-directed accounts (see below).

In many circumstances, participants have the option of borrowing money from the plan. This action should probably be viewed as a last resort under only the most dire financial circumstances. Borrowing from the plan requires strict adherence to several complex rules which, if violated, may result in a required loan repayment prior to its normal maturity date. The participant might also have to pay an excise tax to the government plus get taxed on the loan itself. (For more about participant loans, see Part IV, Section C.)

K. Selecting Service Providers for Your Plan

Most businesses, whether small or large, recognize that the various rules and requirements with respect to retirement plans are simply too complicated for them to administer on their own. For this reason, most companies will at some point or another hire several outside service providers to help them with the design, legal, record keeping, and investment aspects of their plan.

How do you go about finding or selecting a qualified service provider? Well, as with many things, there is no one correct answer to this question. However, we do have a number of suggestions:

- It always helps to talk to other business people to see which TPAs, employee benefits attorneys, investment advisors, etc., they use and with whom they are happy.

- Whenever selecting any of these service providers, always interview at least two or three and compare their qualifications, as well as their fees.

- Always request and check the references for all prospective service providers.

- Make sure that any service provider that you are considering can demonstrate a significant degree of experience in working with your type of plan and your type of company. You do not want a service provider "learning" about ERISA or about employee benefit plans at your expense.

- Once you hire any outside service provider, make sure you have a definite agreement with that service provider, which spells out the services they will provide, the fees they will charge (and how these fees will be paid), as well as spelling out the parties' relative responsibilities for certain compliance requirements. For example, if you, the plan administrator (not the TPA) will be responsible for the actual mailing of the plan's annual report to the IRS (Form 5500), you should make sure that this is spelled out either as part of the agreement or as part of some checklist that you receive from your advisor. By making sure that there is complete and well-documented correspondence regarding these kinds of responsibilities, you will avoid missing deadlines and having compliance obligations "fall through the cracks."

- Perhaps one of the most fundamental requirements for any advisor to your business is the requirement that you "trust" your advisor's abilities and judgment. If, at any time, you lose confidence in your advisor's abilities or judgment, you should feel free to obtain a second opinion or you should consider finding a new advisor.

ACTION: *If you are an overburdened plan sponsor, trustee, or personnel manager, you should figure out ways to use others to simplify plan operations. Possibilities include:*

1. *Hire a third party administrator to help you administer the plan and get it out of your office;*

2. *Hire an investment consultant or manager to help with your investments;*

3. *Hire an employee benefits attorney to help with any plan design and operational problems; or*

4. *Have your in-house administrator work more closely with your TPA and/or investment broker to make the plan investments easier to administer.*

If you are interested in letting your employees direct the investment of their own accounts, make sure that you discuss the pros and cons of this change with your TPA, employee benefits attorney, and investment advisor.

Part IV.
The Rules of the Road

The contents of this part of the survival guide are:

A. The Government's Watchful Eyes—The IRS, DOL, and PBGC

Traveling on today's modern highways is safer because of the various traffic laws in place to protect us along the way. The highway patrol and local law enforcement agencies are always patrolling the roadways and making sure that we comply with these laws.

Similarly, the journey to retirement has been made safer for participants because of the guidelines provided primarily by ERISA. The law enforcement agencies who patrol the roads to retirement are:

1. The Internal Revenue Service (IRS)

The IRS is responsible for enforcing the income tax aspects of retirement plans. A major emphasis here is upon ensuring that plans are not weighted so heavily in favor of highly compensated employees that workers with lower incomes are underserved. The IRS has the authority to audit a plan in order to enforce its regulations.

2. The United States Department of Labor (DOL)

The DOL is responsible for labor law aspects of retirement plans, which are primarily designed to ensure that they pay the benefits promised. They are also responsible for making sure that plans are described accurately. Like their tax-related cohorts, agents of the DOL also have authority to investigate the plan.

3. The Pension Benefit Guaranty Corporation (PBGC)

The PBGC is a branch of the DOL that administers the termination insurance program mandated by ERISA for certain defined benefit plans only. The PBGC is responsible for guaranteeing certain minimum benefits to participants in defined benefit plans that are not exempt from its jurisdiction. Employers who sponsor such plans pay premiums to the PBGC, much like your driver in the mountains pays a special insurance fee to protect against the peril of uninsured motorists. If the plan is subject to PBGC jurisdiction, it must follow specific PBGC rules and requirements regarding plan termination. Under certain extreme circumstances, the PBGC has the authority to assume control of a retirement plan if the plan is in danger, much the same as the FSLIC can take over an ailing savings and loan.

B. Government Reports and Compliance

In order to assist the government in enforcing the rules and to promote voluntary compliance by employers, plans must file reports with the government agencies listed above.

1. Reporting to the IRS

The plan administrator must file the following reports with the IRS:

- An annual return/report must be filed on a Form 5500, Form 5500-C, Form 5500-R, or Form 5500-EZ (all commonly referred to as the Form 5500). A Form 5500 must be filed for each plan, including plans which have been frozen, generally within seven months following each plan year end. This filing with the IRS also satisfies the DOL's annual filing requirement.

- If distributions were made to participants or beneficiaries during the year, the amounts distributed and any income taxes withheld must be reported on a Form 1099-R.

- Similarly, if the plan buys life insurance for the benefit of any participant, a Form 1099-R must be filed setting forth the value of the life insurance protection (commonly known as the "P. S. 58 cost").

- If the plan merges or consolidates with another plan or transfers assets to another plan, a Form 5310-A may have to be filed (unless the exceptions set forth on the form are satisfied).

In addition, the following filings are optional, but generally recommended:

- When the plan is started or the documents are amended, a Form 5300 series application may be filed with the IRS for a favorable letter of determination on the plan's documents. Although not required, such a filing is advisable because you can receive confirmation from the IRS that your plan documents are in compliance with the applicable law.[1]

- When the plan is terminated, a Form 5310 is generally filed as part of an application for determination from the IRS concerning the termination of a plan (the failure to get such approval may increase the likelihood of an audit by the IRS).

The trustees may also have to file a Form 990T with the IRS if the plan has UBTI. Also, if there are excise taxes (e.g., a prohibited transaction has occurred or the employer has failed to meet a plan's minimum funding requirements), a Form 5330 should be filed with the IRS.

2. Reporting to the DOL

Unless the plan is specifically exempt from the reporting and disclosure requirements of ERISA, as would be the case with a one-participant plan covering only the owner of the company, the following reports must generally be filed with the DOL:

---

[1]In many cases, it is possible to use a standardized prototype plan. If your company can utilize one of these, it is generally not necessary to apply for a determination letter.

- The annual return/report (Form 5500) filed with the IRS fulfills the DOL annual filing requirement.

- When the plan is started, a copy of the plan's summary plan description (SPD) must be filed with the DOL. Quite simply, this document outlines the various features of the plan in plain language for the participants and identifies the specific benefits to which they are entitled.

- As the plan is modified, summary descriptions of plan modifications must be filed with the DOL.

3. Reporting to the PBGC

If a defined benefit plan is subject to PBGC reporting, it's required to file PBGC Form-1 on an annual basis and pay an appropriate PBGC premium along with such filing. In addition, if the plan encounters funding problems, a report must be filed with the PBGC. It may also be necessary to notify the PBGC when certain "reportable events" happen with respect to your defined benefit plan.

C. Watching for Trouble Along the Way

On any journey there are potential hazards. Normally, the major ones are well defined by signs posted prominently along the route so that you can avoid them. Similarly, plan fiduciaries are warned to stay away from certain territory and to keep off certain routes unless special governmental authorization is obtained in advance. These road hazards are called "prohibited transactions" which must be "corrected" (usually that means undoing the deal) and frequently result in the payment of excise taxes.

1. Prohibited Transactions Generally

A transaction is prohibited when a plan enters into a transaction with a "disqualified person" or a "party in interest," which would include:

- A person who has any authority over plan management or investments;

- A person who provides services to the plan;

- The employer;

- A corporation or partnership which is 50 percent or more owned by any of the first three categories;

- Anyone who owns 50 percent or more of the company;

- A person who is a member of the family of any of the above;

- Certain officers, directors, shareholders, and employees; and

- A person who is a 10 percent or more partner of certain persons described above.

Examples of prohibited transactions with any of those identified above include:

- Selling or leasing any property to the retirement plan (e.g., the plan's majority shareholder and his wife lease a piece of property owned by the plan or the employer contributes property to the plan);

- Borrowing money or receiving any other extension of credit from the plan (e.g., the president of ABC Tractor deposits plan assets in a bank and the bank then lends the money to the company for an equipment purchase);

- Furnishing goods, facilities, or services to the plan (e.g., the company sponsoring the plan provides space for plan administration activities and charges rent to the plan);

- Transferring or using plan assets for the fiduciary's own use (e.g., Dr. Jones uses pension money to purchase land upon which he later intends to build a vacation home);

- Entering the plan into questionable business arrangements in order to secure advantageous terms in private transactions (e.g., plan funds are deposited in a bank's low-yield savings account in exchange for the bank's agreement to loan money to the company's president); and

- A fiduciary receiving consideration for his or her own personal account from a party dealing with the plan (e.g., the chief financial officer of a company agrees to use a brokerage house to invest plan assets and receives discount trading on his own account as their little way of saying thank you).

In some situations, the DOL will grant exemptions from the prohibited transaction rules. Such exemptions include class exemptions on which all those who come within its terms may rely and individually granted exemptions which require a special application to be made.

Sometimes a transaction that appears to be on the up-and-up might be considered illegal by the government because the regulators apply a broad definition of what constitutes "plan assets." For example, under certain circumstances, a plan's investment in the stock of a corporation or as a partner in a partnership causes not only the investment itself to be an asset of the plan, but the assets owned by that corporation or partnership may also be considered to be plan assets. If a disqualified person deals with such a corporation or partnership, the transaction may be prohibited.

2. Participant Loans

The prohibited transaction rule that is most often encountered by plan fiduciaries involves plan loans to participants. A loan to a participant is a prohibited transaction unless the loan satisfies each of the following criteria:

- Loans are available to all participants on a reasonably equivalent basis;

- Loans are not available to highly compensated employees in a greater amount than to other participants;

- Loans are made in accordance with specific provisions regarding such loans set forth in the plan;

- The loan bears a reasonable rate of interest;

- The loan is adequately secured; and

- The loan is not made to a sole proprietor, a more than 10 percent partner, or a more than 5 percent shareholder of an S corporation, as defined by the Internal Revenue Code.

If a participant loan is a prohibited transaction and the loan is secured by the participant's benefit under the plan, not only do you have to deal with the resulting excise taxes, you might even face disqualification of the entire plan.

Even if the loan isn't a prohibited transaction, there will be adverse income tax consequences to the participant if the loan is treated as a "deemed distribution." If (1) the loan exceeds a statutory dollar limit (e.g., $50,000), or (2) the loan doesn't require repayment within five years (certain home loans are exempt from this five-year requirement), or (3) the loan doesn't require that principal and interest payments be made at least quarterly, or (4) the participant doesn't repay the loan according to its terms, then all or part of the loan will be included in the participant's gross income and the plan should issue a Form 1099-R to the participant for the amount of the deemed distribution.

If a loan is treated as a deemed distribution under these rules, the loan is not actually treated as a distribution for plan qualification purposes unless the plan forecloses on the loan security and extinguishes the debt. If such foreclosure occurs prior to the time when the plan could make an actual distribution to the borrowing participant, the plan may be disqualified. If there's no extinguishment of the debt, the loan must still be repaid even though the participant has been taxed on all or part of the loan. Repayments to a plan on such a loan are treated as voluntary nondeductible contributions to the plan. These amounts are not taxed again when they are subsequently distributed to the participant.

Consider this nightmare situation: Freddie's Elm Street Garage, Inc. maintains a defined contribution plan that permits participant loans. Freddie has an account balance of $200,000 and Freddie decides to borrow $100,000 secured by his account balance under the plan (which exceeds the plan's $50,000 loan limit). Freddie decides to repay the loan on an interest-only basis with a balloon payment at the end of ten years. What are the consequences? Freddie has violated both the prohibited transaction rules (such a loan was not allowed by the plan documents), thereby risking the qualified status of the plan, and the deemed distribution rules resulting in $100,000 of gross income. To make matters worse, in an effort to rectify the situation, Freddie repays $50,000 of the loan by transferring his Krugerrand collection to the plan, thereby engaging in another prohibited transaction (the exchange of his property in cancellation of the debt) and has caused the plan to invest in a collectible which may result in additional gross income and penalties for Freddie.

D. Adequate Insurance

1. ERISA Fiduciary Bonds

Most of us are aware that uninsured motorists are a hazard on the road. We are required to maintain certain minimum insurance coverage and we may pay additional premiums or taxes to fund an uninsured motorists pool. Similarly, the drivers of retirement plans (the fiduciaries) are subject to certain minimum insurance requirements.

In general, every fiduciary, as well as anyone who handles funds or other property of the plan, must be bonded. Certain entities (e.g., banks, savings and loans, trust companies, insurance companies) may be exempt from the bonding requirements. These bonding requirements include:

- The bond must cover at least 10 percent of the amount handled by the bonded individual (e.g., if the person handles plan assets of $200,000, the bond must be at least $20,000);

- The bond may not be for less than $1,000 (e.g., even if the plan's assets are less than $10,000, the bond must be for $1,000); and

- The bond need not be for more than $500,000 (e.g., even if the plan assets exceed $5,000,000, the bond needs to be only for $500,000).

One bond can cover every fiduciary in the company. Bonding can be purchased through a casualty insurance broker either by purchasing an individual bond (sometimes called an "ERISA bond") or by adding a rider to existing liability coverage.

2. PBGC Insurance Premiums (Defined Benefit Plans Only)

The plan administrators of certain retirement plans must pay premiums to the PBGC, which is responsible for guaranteeing certain minimum benefits to participants in defined benefit plans under its jurisdiction. Generally, only defined benefit plans that are maintained exclusively for substantial owners of the business or that are maintained by small professional businesses (no more than 25 participants) are exempt from the PBGC's jurisdiction. If a plan subject to the PBGC's jurisdiction cannot pay the benefits promised, the PBGC will pay minimum benefits to the participants. The PBGC may then pursue a claim against the employer for its expenses.

3. Fiduciary Liability Insurance

Some of us don't feel that our normal insurance offers enough coverage in case of a claim against us. To cover this contingency, we purchase additional insurance or an umbrella policy. Similarly, plan fiduciaries may desire to obtain fiduciary liability insurance for themselves. Such coverage is optional and the policies are often quite expensive and may be narrowly drawn. Before a fiduciary or a plan sponsor decides to purchase such insurance, it's important to evaluate the extent of coverage, the exclusions from coverage, and the overall cost/benefit of providing such coverage. This coverage may be very beneficial in the event that someone accuses the fiduciaries of shirking their responsibilities, through such actions as mismanagement, misinvestment of the funds, improper handling of trust assets, etc.

ACTION: *If you have any problems with compliance, contact an employee benefits attorney for advice and help with solving the problem.*

Part V.

On the Road

The contents of this part of the survival guide are:

It's not a good idea to embark on a long journey without some advance planning. Surprise, surprise! It is good sense to map out where you want to go, how you are going to get there, who is going to do the driving, and benchmarks along the way in order to determine if you are on course and on schedule.

In order to maximize your chances of achieving your retirement goals it's essential to "map" out the investment strategy for your retirement savings. This calls for a written investment policy which describes where you are, where you want to end up (in terms of investment performance), and how you plan to get there.

A. The Investment Policy

Every plan should have a written investment policy statement. Depending on your retirement plan's funding goals and how much time you have to achieve them, your investment policy should be developed through a process of evaluating needs, determining risk tolerances, and establishing a program of prudent management and investment monitoring. This policy should be clear and specific enough to be followed by yourself and any investment advisors or managers you select. Broad-based generalities should be avoided since, as investment goals and objectives, they mean different things to different people.

At a minimum, the following items should be covered when designing an investment policy statement:

- The statement should set a desired annual rate of return. There are two types of returns to consider:

    1. The absolute rate of return such as 8 percent over a three-year time period;

    2. The relative rate of return, such as 5 percent over inflation. If inflation is 3 percent, the desired relative rate of return would be 8 percent. If inflation were 6 percent, the desired relative rate of return would be 11 percent. This rate of return is easier to use over time as inflation and market conditions change.

Many people wonder what rates are reasonable to be in their policy statement. The following table referencing the period from 1926 to 1995 is included to give you some reference points with respect to historical rates of return. For example, a portfolio mix of 50 percent S&P index stocks and 50 percent intermediate-term bonds would historically have averaged 7.65 percent. With inflation of 3.10 percent, that would be a relative return of 4.55 percent over inflation.

Annual Compound Returns[1]

	1926-1995	1980s	1990-1995
Common Stocks/S&P 500	10.5%	17.5%	13.0%
Small Company Stocks	12.5%	15.8%	15.3%
Long-Term Corporate Bonds	5.0%	13.0%	11.3%
Intermediate-Term Govt. Bonds	5.0%	11.9%	9.0%
U.S. Treasury Bills	3.7%	8.9%	4.9%
Inflation	3.1%	5.1%	3.4%

As you can see, the 1980s were historically high relative to the long-term returns and are not a good benchmark. The 1980s were the best decade ever in bonds and the second-best decade for stocks. The 1926-1995 returns are a good long-term benchmark.

- The statement should specify how often there should be a review and evaluation of the plan's investment performance, such as annually or quarterly.

- Allowable investments and quality standards should be delineated. Examples: corporate bonds will have no lower than an "A" rating, U.S. stocks purchased must be included in the S&P 500 index, only unleveraged real estate can be purchased, and first deeds of trust must have no higher than a 50 percent loan-to-value ratio.

- Liquidity requirements, such as a percent of the portfolio, should be set.

- It's important to keep the assets properly diversified to guard against unacceptable losses caused by major downturns in any one area. This maxim is widely known, even among casual investors, and is particularly crucial in retirement planning because success or failure can have far-reaching effects.

- Cash flow of the plan is both inflow and outflow, and should be stated. For example, $30,000 is expected to be added yearly.

- If money managers are hired, there should be procedures for selecting and dismissing them and monitoring their performance, as well as specifying how they will be paid.

- Once a policy is set, it should be reviewed at least annually to assure that the plan is in compliance and that the policy is modified as necessary in order to reflect changes within the plan or the economy.

[1]Source: 1995 Yearbook, Ibbotson Associates.

B. Who Should Drive?

An investment management structure must be set up by the employer. The two options are:

- A management system for all funds;
- Participants directing their individual accounts.

1. A Management System for All Funds

The employer, as we mentioned, has the option of either managing the plan's investments directly or appointing someone else to do so. A selection must be made among the following:

a. Active Self-Trustees

The trustees of the retirement plan can be the principals of the business who function as both trustees and investment managers. The trustees set up and oversee the investment of the retirement plan's assets, monitor performance of the plan, make investment changes as necessary, and report the performance of the investments to the plan administrator (which role they may also fulfill).

If you do not have considerable experience with investing trust assets, you should hire an investment advisor to assist you in selecting the proper investments in accordance with your investment policy. An investment advisor can give you advice on many money management issues such as overall retirement planning, estate planning, tax planning, insurance, and portfolio management. You can locate a financial advisor by checking with:

- Independent financial planning firms;
- Stockbrokerage firms;
- Insurance agencies;
- Banks, savings and loans, and credit unions.

b. Third-Party Trustee

The trustee of the retirement plan can also be any other individual or entity that is qualified and willing to be a trustee (e.g., a bank's trust department). Using a third-party trustee shifts some of ERISA's legal responsibilities away from the business owner. As would be the case where the principals of the business act as the trustees, here again the third-party trustee can act as both the trustee and the investment manager, or the investment management duties may be delegated to another, in which case the trustee would be merely a custodian of the plan's assets.

c. Investment Manager

Another option is to hire an outside professional manager to assist with part of the responsibilities or offer expert advice along the way. The trustees of the plan may also delegate the responsibility of money management to one or more investment managers, thus making their own major responsibility a matter of overseeing the manager.

The advantages of appointing an investment manager are:

- The investment professional is trained and experienced in portfolio management, and might be more qualified to do the job than the trustees themselves;
- The job of monitoring the manager can be less time-consuming than managing the assets;
- The investment professional shares the liability for the plan's investment performance.

The disadvantages, on the other hand, are:

- The investment manager's approach may be highly sophisticated and more difficult for the trustees to understand, thus making it more difficult for the trustees to determine whether the manager is doing a good job;
- The trustees may have the tendency to neglect their responsibility for monitoring plan investments, thinking that the investment manager is taking care of everything.

If you turn over the investment planning to a third party, you will remain liable for that person's actions. However, ERISA contains a special rule that allows you to select a professional who meets certain minimum requirements and can bear a substantial portion of that responsibility. Under this rule, the investment manager must be one of the following and acknowledge in writing that he or she is a fiduciary of your plan, if this person or institution is expected to absorb liability:

- A "registered investment advisor" under the Investment Advisers Act of 1940;
- A bank; or
- An insurance company.

Choosing your investment manager should be done carefully. You should select someone with a good reputation and a proven track record. In any event, don't forget to keep an eye on their performance.

What every business owner, or plan sponsor, should know before they attempt to take on the task of investing retirement plan funds for themselves is that the Department of Labor has maintained that "any fiduciary involved in the investment of plan assets is charged with the responsibility to invest those assets with the skills of a professional." So, in other words, if anyone is going to manage the assets themselves, they had better be an expert or otherwise hire one.

We've seen too many plans that have been managed improperly. The business owner, busy with the task of running the business, leaves the investment decision making to their CFO or human resources department. Investment mismanagement also happens when investment decisions are turned over to unskilled investment brokers or sales personnel. Both of these situations are mistakes! Take the responsibility for selecting an investment manager seriously and don't try to do it yourself unless you consider yourself an expert.

2. Paying Someone Else to Drive

If you decide to hire a financial advisor or an investment manager to assist you with the management of your plan's investment portfolio, you need to know a little about how these advisors get paid.

a. Fee Only

Fees include an hourly rate for consultation or an annual fee to manage an investment portfolio. Usually a portfolio management fee is a yearly percentage of assets managed. Fees could run 1 percent to 3 percent on a portfolio of $100,000, decreasing for larger portfolios.

b. Commission Only

Stockbrokers, insurance agents, and financial planners may work for the commissions they earn from investments that you place with them. Sometimes this amount is obvious, such as a 4 percent commission charged to buy a mutual fund. At times the amount isn't so obvious. For example:

- Stocks and bonds have different buy and sell commission amounts. Ask your broker to disclose what your commissions are each time you place a trade and as a percent average monthly or annually.

- Mutual funds and annuities that may appear to be "no-load" at times have either a higher than normal yearly fee and/or an exit fee if you sell the investment before five to eight years. Be sure you understand any surrender charges or annual charges that apply.

c. Fee and Commission

Some advisors charge a fee for the initial consultation and/or the yearly planning work, as well as brokering investments that have commissions. There can be advantages and disadvantages to this arrangement.

- **Advantages:** If the advisor has a broad range of investment choices and isn't a captive agent to just a select group of choices, they could provide expert advice on the best options available.

- **Disadvantages:** This arrangement has the most potential for conflicts of interest. Are you paying a fee to be steered only into options which provide additional compensation to the advisor? Will there be any recommendations given by the advisor that can be implemented without going through him or her?

Another variation of the fee and commission arrangement is for the advisor to offset the fee against any commissions generated. So, if investments or insurance products are purchased, this could be essentially a commission-only arrangement.

3. Participants Directing Their Individual Accounts

Defined contribution plans (but not defined benefit plans) can allow participants to direct their own investment accounts. If this is done properly, the fiduciary responsibility of the trustees will be reduced.

In many cases the trustees will determine the list of investment options from which the participants will be allowed to choose. The trustees must offer a diverse selection of investment options that are good performers. A few high-risk, potential big-gainers may also be on the "menu." If the participant feels particularly sporting, substantially higher rewards can be gained. But if the participant makes a wrong turn in the high-risk options, the participant alone may be responsible for the loss.

Okay, now the downside:

- If the individual employees are unfamiliar with investment management and its risks, the total return could be less than expected;

- If each participant has at least three choices, as required by law, and has his or her own individual account (as opposed to a part of one large pool), the volume of paperwork may multiply accordingly (unless certain types of investment options are used); and

- A limited number of choices may not offer sufficient diversification at the participant level.

Section 404(c) of ERISA provides guidance in this area. Under this provision, plan fiduciaries can avoid liability for plan losses and participants will be deemed to have exercised control over their assets in their accounts when certain conditions are satisfied. A participant must have the opportunity to:

- Choose from a broad range of investment alternatives that may materially affect the potential return on assets;

- Give investment instructions with the frequency that is appropriate in light of investment volatility, such as the stock and bond markets; and

- Obtain sufficient information to make informed investment decisions.

The details for operating such a program can be found in the regulations published by the DOL. Although this approach is popular and sounds simple, the regulations are complex.

The trustees must ensure that none of the transactions made through the plan break any laws. For example, a plan subject to ERISA may not loan money to the employer without an exemption granted by the DOL.

Although employers may allow the plan to loan money to participants, strict rules must be followed. In the event of any discovered illegal transactions, the transaction must be corrected, penalties must be paid to the government in the form of excise taxes, and the trustees are held accountable for any lost funds. Trustees, by the way, may never borrow money from the fund, unless it's from their own account.

Even if the plan allows participants to direct the investment of their own accounts, the trustees may be held personally liable if it's determined that they invested retirement fund monies recklessly or otherwise shirked their responsibilities. For this reason, some employers want others, such as RIAs, to assist the trustees and participants. In such cases, the responsibility for investing plan assets may be shifted from the trustees to others.

C. Investment Principles

Those charged with the responsibility for driving a vehicle must drive the vehicle safely and effectively. If they go too fast, there are risks. If they make high-risk investments, the trustees could soon face a lot of angry people and government agents with a lot of questions. If risky investments are made and money is lost, a crash happens. The drivers (trustees) may be held liable to the passengers (participants) for the damages. If they go too slow, there are risks as well. The passengers (employees) will not reach their destinations on time. If only interest-bearing accounts are used, the assets may grow at a guaranteed 5 percent annual rate versus a stock fund that historically has realized a 10 percent annual rate, but has risk. Keep in mind, however, that $100,000 earning 5 percent more over 20 years is an additional $400,000.

The risk tolerance of the trustees and the length of time you have to generate sufficient funds for payout are two highly important variables that will likely be unique to your particular situation. Such guidelines are generally set by the trustees as a means of providing direction to the financial advisors. There are no perfect investments and no definite rules for choosing this direction. So, it's best to rely on some basic principles that will help keep the plan on track and secure.

Our traffic laws have a basic principle of safety behind them. The retirement plan counterpart is found in the following ERISA rules:

• The "exclusive benefit rule" can be viewed as the great truism of ERISA. Every other restriction and guideline leads back to this big one, which mandates that each of the fiduciaries discharge his duties solely in the interests of plan participants and beneficiaries. Any other goals or objectives of the fiduciaries must not interfere with this purpose.

• Each of the fiduciaries must discharge his duties with care, skill, prudence, and diligence, addressing the existing circumstances in a reasonable manner ("prudent expert" rule). Improper action or inaction can be highly dangerous. In other words, if our friend zooming up the mountain sees a large boulder on the road, choices include stopping to push it out of the way, steering around it, or trying a different route. Blindly slamming into the obstruction has serious repercussions. The same is true in investment planning. Fiduciaries can get in almost as much trouble for ignoring obvious problems as they can for illegal acts.

• The fiduciaries must diversify the plan's investments in order to minimize the risk of large losses from an unexpected downturn. If, however, circumstances are such that it's clearly (and the key word is clearly) prudent not to diversify, then you need not diversify.

D. Investment Choices—Risk and Reward

There is a multitude of investment choices to use in your retirement plan that will be described in this chapter. We liken them to engines that can be used to power your retirement plan vehicle.

A mainstream type of investment program would be similar to a four cylinder engine. A four cylinder engine produces average power to navigate most inclines along your route towards your retirement goal. It is also very fuel efficient and produces consistent output for the fuel used. This would be the type of conservative to moderate risk portfolios described in Part V, Section E.3.

An aggressive investment program is like a six cylinder engine. The owner of the six cylinder engine wants to drive faster than most other people on the road. He wants to get to his destination quicker and he wants to get around those curves faster and climb faster. Sure, it might be less fuel effective, but the thrill is worth it. This investor would like the aggressive portfolio described in Part V, Section E.3.

The very aggressive investor uses a V-8 or V-12 engine. He wants all the power he can get to speed himself along the regular streets, go on country roads or to accelerate up hills and mountains. This is a high risk venture as this investor could get to his destination way before anyone else but there is a danger that he could strain these high horsepower engines and blow them up. This investor doesn't like standard stock and bond portfolios. He might pick a new stock just going on the stock market and bet 25 percent of his portfolio on this stock. His motto is "Win big or lose big—I'm going for it." This could work but the probability is high that this investor will violate the prudent investor rules set up by ERISA.

There's usually a direct correlation between risk and reward when it comes to making these choices. The more risk taken, the more potential for reward and vice versa. For example, there's little to no risk to money deposited in a bank, but there is a limited return. Although this type of account would never double its value in three years, as is possible in some equity investments, it's also never in danger of loss of principal as long as it's within FDIC insurance limits.

The two main types of investments are:

• **Fixed Assets**
Money invested in interest-bearing accounts that usually have a maturity date. Examples are bank accounts, government bonds, corporate bonds, and loans on real estate or to participants.

• **Equity Assets**
Money invested in an asset that is owned by the retirement plan with no guarantee of a fixed return. However, the return may be higher than fixed assets. On the other hand, you could own a worthless investment. Examples are U.S. stocks, foreign stocks, and real estate.

Figure 1 (page 50) shows a number of asset classes along a risk/reward continuum. (F) refers to a fixed asset, (E) refers to an equity asset. As you can see, most (F) fixed assets are lower risk/lower reward and most (E) equity assets are higher risk/higher reward.

1. How Does One Reduce Risk and Achieve a Targeted Return?

• Know that time is your friend. Figure 2 (page 50) shows the extreme ranges of yearly returns on stocks and how time evens out the returns and reduces the volatility. An investor who is educated about the long-term track record of stocks will have the perspective and the patience to wait out the down periods.

• Diversify your portfolio among different asset classes.

• "Allocate" your assets according to your investment philosophy and investment policy. Asset allocation is the practice of using certain blends of investments together to achieve certain rates of return with an acceptable degree of investment risk.

Asset Classes & Risk

Annualized returns for 10 years
Ending 12/31/95

Higher Return ↑

Lower Return

■ Venture Capital (E) ....*
■ Small Cap. Stocks (E) 11.9%
■ International Stocks (E) 13.6%
■ Large Cap. Equity (E) 14.5%
■ Convertibles (E) 10.1%
■ High Yield Bonds (F) 11.5%
■ Real Estate (E) ....*
■ Long-Term Corporate Bonds (F) 11.3%
■ Intermediate Gov't Bonds (F) 9.1%
■ Short-Term Bonds (F) ....*
■ Cash Equivalents (F) 5.6%

Lower Risk ◄──────► Higher Risk

* No measure available   Returns from Morningstar and Ibbotson Associates

Figure 1

Range of Yearly Returns on Stocks

For various time periods 1941-90, with dividends reinvested

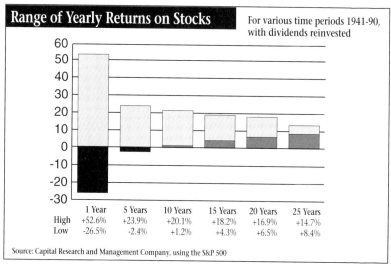

	1 Year	5 Years	10 Years	15 Years	20 Years	25 Years
High	+52.6%	+23.9%	+20.1%	+18.2%	+16.9%	+14.7%
Low	-26.5%	-2.4%	+1.2%	+4.3%	+6.5%	+8.4%

Source: Capital Research and Management Company, using the S&P 500

Figure 2

The 1990 Nobel Prize in economics resulted from a 40-year study demonstrating that **less than 10 percent** of investment return is attributable to individual stock selection. See chart on page 51.

Allocation of investments between equities, bonds, and cash accounts is the single most important determinant of investment success. It also can be the most time-consuming part of the investment process. There are two styles of asset allocation:

- A mix of many different assets so that the combination of assets produces a higher return with less risk. Computer models and consultants have become very sophisticated in developing an ideal mix of assets based on historical performance figures.

1.7% Timing
2.2% Other
4.6% Individual Asset Selection
91.5% Asset Class

- Determining the best asset classes to be in at various times and changing asset classes as economic conditions change. For example, oil, gold, and real estate were asset classes that produced some of the most favorable returns in the 1970s. In the 1980s, stocks and bonds produced the best results. Which assets will prove to be the best in the years ahead? Since many people feel incapable of getting a good answer to this question, they resort to the first style and invest in a mix of many different types of assets.

2. Diversification Examples

a. Fixed Assets and Equity Assets

If you put 50 percent of your money in a 6 percent Treasury note maturing in five years, you will have no risk since you will get all of your money back in five years, along with 6 percent yearly interest. If you compare that with the other 50 percent in a stock mutual fund with a good past track record, you would expect it could return somewhere around 10 percent, the historical average, after holding it five years. The stock fund has less certainty, but greater upside potential, than your 6 percent Treasury note. Your expected composite return would be 8 percent (50 percent at 6 percent, 50 percent at 10 percent).

b. U.S. Stocks and Foreign Stocks

You can diversify a stock risk by having some money in U.S. stocks and some money in foreign stocks, perhaps an international mutual fund where the manager has stocks in many foreign countries. In years when the U.S. stock market is down, there's a possibility that the foreign markets may be up. In 1994, both U.S. and foreign stocks were low. However, in 1987, the U.S. S&P 500 stock index was +5.2 percent and foreign funds were up on average +12.9 percent.

c. Different Types of U.S. Stocks

Large company stocks, such as those traded on the New York Stock Exchange, have been in existence longer and have bigger product lines and sales than smaller, newer companies generally found on the NASDAQ stock exchange. The smaller compa-

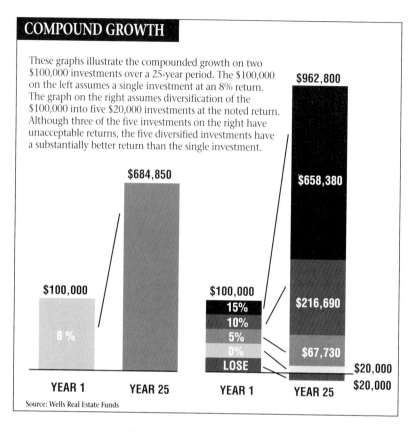

COMPOUND GROWTH

These graphs illustrate the compounded growth on two $100,000 investments over a 25-year period. The $100,000 on the left assumes a single investment at an 8% return. The graph on the right assumes diversification of the $100,000 into five $20,000 investments at the noted return. Although three of the five investments on the right have unacceptable returns, the five diversified investments have a substantially better return than the single investment.

$962,800

$684,850

$658,380

$100,000
8 %

$100,000
15%
10%
5%
0%
LOSE

$216,690

$67,730

$20,000
$20,000

YEAR 1   YEAR 25   YEAR 1   YEAR 25

Source: Wells Real Estate Funds

nies, generally speaking, have greater growth potential and greater risk. The 1926-1995 historical average is 10.2 percent for the S&P 500 stock index and 12.2 percent for small company stocks. In the 1980s the S&P 500 averaged 17.5 percent and small company stocks averaged 15.5 percent. So this relationship doesn't always exist. In the last five years ending December 31, 1995, the relationship is back as the S&P 500 achieved 13 percent versus small companies at 15.3 percent. Thus, diversification among these two groups can be effective.

The chart above shows an example of different rates of return achieved on a diversified portfolio over a 25-year period. It graphically shows how you can be effective even if all of your investments don't perform.

E. Investing Plan Assets—How to Get Started!

So you've just started out on the exciting journey of choosing investments that fit the goals of your retirement plan. What's the first step?

1. Answer Vital Questions

Before the actual investments are chosen, answer these questions:

- What type of a plan do you have?
- How much will go into the plan the first year?
- What's the expected annual investment in the plan?
- What's your expected rate of return?
- What amount of downside on an investment can you tolerate?
- Can your participants tolerate seeing negative rates of return?
- How close or far away are your employees from retirement?

Remember, every plan should have a written investment policy. Therefore, if you have developed a sound investment policy, most if not all of these questions should have been answered!

2. Determine the Type of Portfolio You Want to Use

Once you've answered the vital questions, you can ascertain how much risk you want to assume. There are three portfolios which illustrate different risk levels. Remember that reward (growth, appreciation) usually increases with more risk. See the annual compound returns table in Part V, Section A, page 42 for historical returns in stocks, bonds, and treasury bills/cash. Stocks have always outperformed bonds over a number of years.

3. Determine the Form of Your Investment

a. Cash

An insured bank account is an easy place to start. Without committing the funds to longer than a year, the trustee should negotiate the highest rate available. Although this is an easy solution, it's not a permanent solution. Remember, leaving funds in an interest-bearing account when the stock or bond market is providing substantially higher returns could leave the trustee or plan sponsor liable to the plan for the difference in return.

b. Mutual Funds

Mutual funds are an easy way to obtain professional management of various types of assets, such as stocks, bonds, or cash. Mutual funds provide diversification and are relatively easy to track for annual rates of return. So, for example, you could have a diversified mutual fund portfolio for as little as $10,000. Depending on your risk tolerance, this might look as follows:

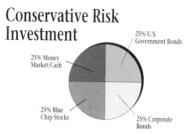

Conservative Risk Investment

25% U.S. Government Bonds
25% Money Market/Cash
25% Blue Chip Stocks
25% Corporate Bonds

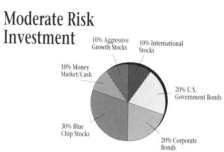

Moderate Risk Investment

10% Aggressive Growth Stocks
10% International Stocks
10% Money Market/Cash
20% U.S. Government Bonds
30% Blue Chip Stocks
20% Corporate Bonds

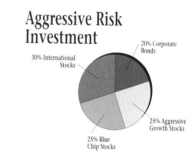

Aggressive Risk Investment

20% Corporate Bonds
30% International Stocks
25% Aggressive Growth Stocks
25% Blue Chip Stocks

Since many mutual funds have a $1,000-$2,500 minimum deposit to start your investment, you can see that you can get a lot of diversification for as little as a $10,000 total portfolio. As the portfolio grows, you can add a second and third family of funds to your investment mix.

The major decision is determining which mutual funds to use. If you decide to select one on your own, you would pick a "no-load" fund that has no commissions paid to a broker. If you decide you need help, you need to select an advisor. See Part V, Section B.2 on compensation methods for details on the variety of methods of payment to advisors.

c. Stocks and Bonds

Individual stocks and bonds can be used. However, because of the size of the portfolio, it may be difficult to obtain adequate diversification. Stocks and bonds can be purchased through a discount broker or a traditional stockbroker. Either way, there is a commission. The difference is the amount and level of ongoing service.

d. Annuity Contract

Another option is an annuity contract. A fixed annuity is an insurance company product invested to receive a fixed rate of return adjusted either monthly, quarterly, semi-annually, or annually. Although it's normally thought that putting an already tax-sheltered investment (such as an annuity) into a retirement plan is like wearing a raincoat indoors, there are times when the certainty of a fixed rate of return and guarantees offered in an annuity contract are appealing to plan trustees. Many times, rates offered through annuity contracts are higher than bank accounts and don't fluctuate in value. However, there are specific areas to investigate:

- The stability of the insurance company is critical, as the insurance company's investments are the security behind the fixed rate of return offered. There are a variety of rating services such as Best and Standard and Poor that show ratings of superior and inferior insurance companies.

- Interest rate history is important to examine for any insurance company. Many times, insurance companies offer a first year "teaser" rate and then the rate falls. Check that the insurance company has a consistent rate renewal history.

A variable annuity is an insurance company investment product offering a choice of investments including multiple money managers or mutual funds invested in U.S. stocks, international stocks, bonds, or government securities. The choice of investment is up to the trustee or the beneficiaries and the return of principal is normally not guaranteed.

- Annuities have no up-front charges, but they have a schedule of surrender charges if the contract is surrendered before five to ten years. Verify the surrender charge schedule on any insurance company contract.

e. Managed Portfolios

Managed portfolios offer several services. They can be thought of as "private" mutual funds that are managed individually for the plan. The assets are managed, invested, and customized for one fee. There are no commissions. They have been called "wrap programs." These programs are offered through investment advisors, stockbrokers, and some banks who are paid directly by the money manager but are employed by the investor. The keys here are the development of an investment strategy and the selection of a manager or managers to carry out that strategy. Therefore, the financial advisor is the key to helping you develop a strategy, choosing the plan's investment manager(s), and providing ongoing monitoring and reporting necessary to determine the effectiveness of the manager at delivering good returns.

4. Participant-Directed Plans

Many defined contribution plans (especially 401(k) plans) are designed to offer investment options to participants for their selection. Determine which option will work best for your employees. For example:

- Three to six funds from one family of mutual funds including a money market fund, a bond fund, and a stock fund; or

- An annuity contract offering options such as a fixed, guaranteed rate fund and a variety of mutual funds from one or many mutual fund families.

It's critical to coordinate the administration of the plan with the investment choices. Work with your administration system or administrator to determine if you will have:

- Pooled accounts where participants make choices among three to six accounts. All investments are "pooled" into each account and the administrator does the bookkeeping to divide the money properly among the participants; or

- Segregated accounts with each participant having his own separate account invested in one or more of the options available.

A prime consideration for selecting an investment provider is the level of service they will provide. At a minimum, the provider should conduct a yearly meeting to update employees on investment performance and to be available to employees to assist them in making the right investment choices for their personal risk tolerance and financial circumstances.

F. Retirement Plan Investments—What Works and What Doesn't?

The world of investments can be overwhelming, but there are some solid guidelines that one should follow when choosing the assets for a retirement plan:

- Choose investments that can be liquidated into cash if necessary without a substantial discount. If a participant leaves the company and distributions need to be made at different times, liquidity of assets is essential. Liquidity means flexibility.

  Examples: Stocks, bonds, CDs, Treasury notes, money market, and mutual funds.

- Choose investments that can be valued on a daily basis. This allows the plan sponsor, the trustees, and the participants the ability to see how the plan is progressing in value. It also assures a fair valuation of assets for distribution purposes when a participant leaves the company.

Examples: Stocks, bonds, CDs, Treasury notes, money market, and mutual funds.

- Stay away from assets that could expose the plan to future liabilities, such as real estate with ongoing maintenance or environmental hazards, and trust deeds that, if in default, may need an outlay of cash in order to be foreclosed.

- Invest in assets on either a stated fee basis (say 1 percent to 2 percent per year for management) or an up-front fee such as that associated with some mutual funds. Avoid paying ongoing "trading commissions" if you have no guarantee of how much they will be each year. ERISA guidelines state that "fees must be reasonable." There's no way to make sure that fees are reasonable unless the trustees know in advance what they are.

- Stay away from limited partnerships. They are difficult to value each year and almost impossible to liquidate without a big discount.

- Consider stocks and stock funds as five- to ten-year investments. The risk and volatility of stocks goes down dramatically when held for at least five years and substantially more at ten years. Stocks also have typically returned 30 percent higher average returns over ten-year periods since 1929.

- Diversify asset classes—don't put all your eggs in one basket, not even if it's a guaranteed bank account. Consider a mix of U.S. stocks, foreign stocks, real estate investment trusts, gold shares, international bonds, U.S. government bonds, U.S. corporate bonds, and specialty stocks for additional diversification.

- Avoid back-end loaded funds or annuities if possible. These are investments that charge a fee if liquidated in the first five to seven years after investment. Statements of value do not reflect these fees. The surprise happens when monies are withdrawn. A participant leaves and gets less than expected or the trustees want to change investments and feel trapped because of the fee charged. Also the ongoing management fees are usually higher on these types of investments.

- Don't invest in already tax-deferred or tax-sheltered investments such as municipal bonds or annuities unless they are designed specifically for pension plans (as are some annuities for 401(k) plans and defined benefit plans).

- Be aware that certain plan investments may result in the payment of income taxes, even though the retirement trust might be otherwise tax exempt, under the unrelated business taxable income (UBTI) rules. If the trust income includes UBTI, the trustees must file income tax returns and pay resulting income taxes. UBTI is triggered by the trust conducting a business, whether directly or through a partnership, and certain leveraged investments. Ascertain that the earnings and growth potential of the investment are strong enough to absorb the extra costs (UBTI tax, accounting costs) to make the investment worth it.

• Keep it simple. Use a system of investments that you can understand and that allows you to review all of the plan assets and calculate the portfolio's return yearly. No matter how sophisticated the investment strategy may be, if it isn't easy to track performance it will become confusing and burdensome to the trustees. Require at least semi-annual, readable statements that show the original investment cost. (See Part VI, Section C, "Evaluating Investment Performance," for more details.)

ACTION: *If you, as a trustee, feel overwhelmed by the investment responsibilities of your plan, consider:*

1. *Hiring a registered investment advisor to assist you in evaluating your investments and designing investment portfolios; or*

2. *Hiring a money manager to manage your portfolio on a daily basis.*

   If your investment performance is inadequate:

1. *Get an investment professional's evaluation of your current investments and suggestions for improvement; or*

2. *Hire money managers with good long-term track records.*

Part VI.

Vehicle Maintenance

The contents of this part of the survival guide are:

Just like an automobile, a retirement plan needs regular servicing and periodic reports on its condition. From time to time, participants leave your company or go through a divorce. In these instances, you need to be aware of the various rules for paying benefits (and dividing benefits between divorcing spouses).

A. Adequate Records Must Be Kept

Plan fiduciaries must maintain plan asset records that will provide sufficient detail for the IRS, the DOL, the PBGC (if applicable), and the participants. The major ones include:

- Asset values at the beginning and end of each plan year;

- Contributions to the plan;

- Distributions from the plan;

- Accounting of all transactions with regard to investments, including purchases, sales, dividends, interest, and shares added;

- Expenses related to investments, such as commissions and sales costs; and

- Records that the administrator (or third party administrator [TPA] if one is hired) will need to complete governmental reports and participant statements.

The plan administrator is required to maintain records relating to all aspects of the plan, from which reports must be filed with the various government agencies mentioned above. A TPA can teach the plan administrator which records, reports, and documents need to be maintained. These records must be accessible for at least six years after the filing date. We advise that you keep all records relating to when employees joined and departed from the plan, as well as details of the amounts of money they withdrew from the plan longer than six years. If possible, it's a good idea to maintain those records throughout the life of the employee or until they have received all of the money to which they are entitled. You never know when someone is going to pick up the phone and start asking questions about their benefits.

The plan administrator must also maintain records to determine any benefits due, in the event of an inquiry by any plan participant who:

- Requests the information (such requests are required to be honored only once in any 12-month period);

- Terminates employment with the company; or

- Has a "break in service," meaning that the individual has performed less than 500 hours of service in a given year.

A plan administrator should maintain the following records:

1. Service

Accurate service records must be kept so that determinations of eligibility, vesting, or benefit accrual may be substantiated. These records should be kept for at least six years, even though the participants have terminated employment and distributions have been made.

2. Compensation

Records of the compensation paid to each participant each year must be maintained for purposes of determining benefits.

3. Benefits

It's important to keep track of benefits for all participants. Requests for information might come not only from the participants, themselves, but also from the DOL or the IRS, which have the right to audit the plan. In addition, certain tests must be performed to ensure that the benefits provided to participants do not exceed the limitations provided by law and that the plan meets the nondiscrimination requirements of the law.

4. Vesting

Accurate records regarding the vested or nonforfeitable interest of each participant must be kept. Sometimes plans become "top heavy," meaning that more than 60 percent of the benefits are going to key employees, such as the business owner. In this case, it may be necessary to maintain records tracking several vesting schedules, because federal laws require shorter vesting schedules during years when the plan is top heavy. An employee who is a participant when the company's plan is top heavy may become vested earlier than usual.

5. Distributions

Records which demonstrate that distributions or payouts to participants have been made in accordance with the various notice, election, and timing requirements of the law must also be retained. For example, when paying benefits to retiring employees, you may have to give the participants at least 30 days' notice (but no more than 90 days) to decide whether they wish to receive their money in the form of an ongoing annuity or as a lump-sum payment. Failure to comply with this notice period could potentially disqualify the entire plan.

The rules governing distributions are numerous and cover a wide variety of issues. Skilled legal advice is a wise investment for these matters.

6. Plan Documents

Dated and executed originals of all plan and trust documents, plan amendments, and copies of all IRS determination letters should be kept on a permanent basis.

B. Establishing the Value of Plan Assets

Plan assets must be valued at "fair market value" periodically, usually yearly, at the end of each plan year (which may not necessarily be December 31). Some guidance is provided in the regulations that govern retirement plans. For example, one regulation (from the Treasury Department) defines "fair market value" as follows:

The fair market value of a plan's assets…is the price at which the property would exchange hands between a willing buyer and a willing seller, neither being under any compulsion to buy nor sell, and both having reasonable knowledge of relevant facts.

Many assets are easy to value, such as cash accounts, stocks, bonds, and mutual funds, all of which have highly accessible market values on the last day of the plan year. Assessing value becomes somewhat more difficult when the assets include real estate and limited partnerships because they are not traded daily. Your investment professional may be able to assist you in gathering this information. Valuation methods available for such assets include:

1. Cost of the Asset

The price paid is especially important when there's no solid evidence that the asset has increased or decreased in value. However, more often than not, the cost of the investment bears no meaningful relationship to the current fair market value of the investment.

2. Appraisal of Current Value

This method is commonly used for real estate, but can be very costly if done yearly. Estimated selling expenses should be deducted from the appraised amount. In the case of limited partnerships, it's often a good idea to prepare a valuation of the partnership which can be used by the plan.

Proper asset valuation is critical. Two examples illustrate this point:

- When the plan guarantees the employee a fixed amount at retirement, any shortfall must be contributed by the employer. Undervalued assets mean the employer pays more than originally planned.

- When the employees receive their account balance at retirement, undervalued or overvalued assets mean they receive too much or too little, while other participants will also be affected in the opposite direction.

C. Evaluating Investment Performance

Plan fiduciaries have to keep an eye on the returns that the invested funds are generating. But, in assessing the level of success, it's important to keep risk tolerance in mind. In other words, your targets and goals must be attainable by the types of assets with which you are comfortable. There's nothing wrong, for example, with seeking the security offered by insured certificates of deposit. The risk of loss is a headache you won't have. But if you choose this road, don't be disappointed if you don't reap double-digit yields!

The following minimum standards should be considered when designing your monitoring process:

- What does your written investment policy say? If you don't have one, you need to stop and develop one right away!

- What are the benchmarks or indices (such as a selected bond index, rate of inflation, prime lending rate, or consumer price index) against which the return on the plan investments will be judged?

- How frequently will investments be reviewed?

- Should lower risk elements in the investment portfolio justify substandard returns?

- How did the investments in the plan perform relative to similar investment portfolios?

- What changes to the plan affected the overall return (i.e., personnel turnover and withdrawal of funds or a change in investment philosophy)?

D. Disclosures to Participants

A copy of the summary plan description (SPD) must be furnished to each participant and beneficiary receiving benefits within 90 days after becoming a participant or first receiving benefits (or within 120 days after a plan is first established). Each participant must also receive updates if the plan is amended. If you hire a TPA, they will help you prepare these disclosures.

Participants are entitled to receive a summary annual report (SAR) within nine months after the close of the plan's fiscal year.

Participants are also entitled to receive notice as interested parties of certain submissions and filings with the IRS. These would include amendments of plans to conform to changes in the law.

Participants must also receive appropriate notice and elections with respect to required withholding of income taxes from any retirement plan distributions as well as appropriate notices and elections with respect to any legally required annuity payments and distributions in excess of $3,500.

The plan administrator must furnish a benefit statement to any plan participant who requests it in writing. However, the participant or beneficiary is entitled to receive only one report during any 12-month period.

If a participant or beneficiary makes a written request for a copy of the SPD, the annual report or plan documents, the plan administrator must comply within 30 days. A reasonable fee to cover the cost of furnishing the requested materials may be charged. A plan administrator who doesn't comply with such requests may become subject to penalties of up to $100 per day from the date the plan administrator fails or refuses to comply.

E. Processing Distributions

The plan administrator is responsible for processing distributions to terminated and retired participants in accordance with applicable law and the plan's provisions. The exact procedure for processing a payout depends upon the type of plan involved and the provisions of the plan document. A TPA often helps the plan administrator with the processing of distributions. The payout itself can take several forms, such as annuities, installments, or lump sums. Retirement benefits that are part of pension plans must also give certain notices and elections to the spouse of a participant before the participant can choose a form of distribution other than a qualified joint and survivor annuity.

Participants will be asked to decide how funds will be paid at the time of retirement. One popular option for taking a distribution is a "direct rollover," meaning that the funds are transferred directly from the plan into an IRA or another qualified plan without actually passing through the hands of the participant. This technique avoids mandatory income tax withholding on the distribution.

All qualified plans are subject to income tax withholding notice and election procedures as well as notice and election procedures regarding the ability of a participant to make a "direct rollover" of his or her benefits to another qualified plan or IRA.

F. Handling Retirement Benefits in Divorce Cases

Retirement benefits are handled somewhat differently when the participant goes through a divorce, and it's highly important for plan administrators to understand the difference in procedure. By law, a plan may not make payment of benefits to the spouse or the participant's children unless a "qualified domestic relations order," or QDRO, is in place.

The plan administrator must establish a written procedure for determining whether a domestic relations order is "qualified" within the meaning of the tax laws and ERISA. When a domestic relations order is received by the plan administrator or the trustees, the plan administrator must notify the participant and the spouse that an order has been received. Furthermore, the plan administrator must advise each party of the procedures under the plan for determining whether the domestic relations order is "qualified." The plan administrator must then determine whether the order is qualified and notify all concerned.

Since the rules regarding qualified domestic relations orders are somewhat complex, and can cause significant problems if not properly followed, the plan administrator should get advice from legal counsel or its TPA with regard to the handling of these orders.

G. Benefit Claims and Appeals

Your plan's procedures for claims and appeals must be specified in writing, with details on what paperwork must be done, how to file appeals, and reasonable time frames. If a claim for benefits is denied, specific provisions of the plan must be cited to support that action, and the participant must again be given details on how to request an appeals hearing. The plan administrator (the same person who made the original finding against the claim) presides over this proceeding and must give the individual sufficient opportunity to introduce evidence or testimony to support their case. All of these determinations (even the decision on appeals) are made by the plan administrator, be it an individual or committee. If the appeal still results in a denial of benefits, the person may then take the matter to court, if desired.

In the event the plan administrator denies a benefit claim, in whole or in part, it's extremely important for the plan administrator to carefully follow the claims procedure and to thoroughly document all of the evidence considered in the initial decision, as well as any decisions on appeal. Such diligence is important because the record of evidence and documentation developed during the claims and appeals process will be useful tools if the participant later files a lawsuit against the plan. In the case of a denied claim, the plan administrator may want to have an employee benefits attorney assist them.

ACTION: *If your investment reports are difficult to understand or you are not getting them regularly or the trustees are not really sure if the return on investments is comparable to similarly invested portfolios:*

1. *Ask the investment manager(s) for a simpler format and to include rates of return for each period covered in the report; or*

2. *Replace the investment advisor.*

See that there's an effective system for keeping employee records so that the plan administrator has the information needed to file accurate reports. This will also help keep administration costs down.

If employees choose their own investments, ask your investment advisor to give annual employee seminars to update their knowledge on investment education and performance.

It's a good idea to check regularly with your TPA and employee benefits attorney to make sure that your plan documents, plan administration procedures, participant disclosures, elections, and forms are current and in compliance with the current rules.

Part VII.

Reaching Your Destination

The contents of this part of the survival guide are:

So, you've finally arrived. You'll be able to enjoy many days of leisure—just a soon as you've done a little pre-retirement planning.

A. Planning for Your Retirement Income

The most fulfilling part of embarking upon a journey is noticing progress along the way and arriving at your destination successfully. But, if each participant relies totally on the contributions made to his company retirement plan without doing his own individual retirement planning, he may have no idea where he stands when he chooses to begin his life of leisure. Every individual should do some personal planning to determine how much he needs to save outside his plan and what rate of return he should try to achieve on his investments.

Chances are there will be a need for extra savings in addition to the retirement vehicle available through employment.

To determine these things, one should review and calculate the following:

1. The amount of income that will be needed at retirement. Use current take-home pay and make adjustments. Will the home mortgage be paid off? Subtract the house payment if it will be paid off. What additional money is needed for travel expenses or health care? Add estimates for these expenses.

2. The amount of income that would be generated by Social Security and the retirement plan.

3. The difference between 1 and 2 above. The shortfall in income may need to come from personal savings or the sale of non-income producing assets such as real estate, your business, or stocks. To make the above calculations include assumptions such as:

   • The inflation rate;

   • Investment return on assets;

   • Exact retirement date; and

   • Life expectancy.

By calculating the above, you, as well as your employees, can plan ahead, knowing what to expect in the way of income from the plan and what provisions need to be made to make up any shortfall.

There's much to consider when choosing a retirement plan for yourself or your company. A basic understanding of the available retirement vehicles and the rules of the road avoid disappointment and breakdowns along the way.

B. Who Should the Beneficiary Be?

Death beneficiary designations should always be current. Care should be taken to assure that the beneficiary designation is coordinated with the overall estate plan of the participant. If the participant is married, the spouse is normally named as the beneficiary. It's usually a mistake to make a living trust the beneficiary of a retirement plan whenever there's a spouse living. The reason? At death, the retirement plan benefits are paid to the living trust, which triggers income tax and generally no rollover election can be made. In addition, the living trust may not be treated as a designated beneficiary for purposes of rules that dictate the timing and amounts of benefit payments that must be paid when the participant reaches age 70½ or dies. Most estate planning experts recommend the primary beneficiary designation be the spouse, with the secondary beneficiary designation being a living trust or other heirs.

The rollover option is then preserved for the spouse, the spouse is the designated beneficiary for required minimum distribution purposes, and the spouse can disclaim the benefits, if appropriate.

C. The Journey's End

How will you be taxed when you take money out of a retirement plan? The money in your retirement plan is fully taxed as income as you take it out. However, some special considerations must be taken into account.

1. Before Age 59½

Distributions received from retirement plans prior to age 59½ are generally subject to a 10 percent federal early distribution penalty tax and perhaps a state tax as well. Therefore, if you take a distribution before age 59½, you must:

- Pay federal (and perhaps state) income taxes;
- Pay a 10 percent federal penalty tax; and
- Perhaps pay a state penalty tax (e.g., 2½ percent in California).

However, you can avoid the penalty taxes if your payments come within one of the exceptions available, such as payments made if you terminate employment after attaining age 55 or you receive substantially equal payments (at least annually) made over your lifetime. Consult your tax advisor on these.

2. Age 59½ or Later

Distributions taken after age 59½ are not subject to these penalty taxes. However, once you have attained age 70½, required minimum distributions must generally begin or you are subject to a 50 percent excise tax on the amount of difference between the required minimum distribution for the year and the amount actually withdrawn.

If the benefit is distributed in a lump sum and after the participant has attained age 59½, the distribution may be eligible for five-year forward averaging (although some taxpayers are eligible for 10-year forward averaging and possibly capital gain treatment). Effective January 1, 2000, five-year averaging will be eliminated.

3. To Rollover or Not to Rollover—That Is the Question

When you retire, leave a place of employment, or discontinue a qualified plan, you must often make a decision. Should you:

a. Take the Money, Pay the Taxes

You can take all or part of the money in a taxable distribution.

Advantages: If you need the funds for a major expenditure, they are available to you. You've paid the taxes at a time when your income may not be as high as it could be later.

If your distribution qualifies, you may be able to use forward income averaging or capital gains treatment in order to lower the effective tax rate on your distribution. The rules governing your eligibility for these special tax benefits can be confusing. It's a good idea for you to discuss them with your CPA or tax attorney.

Disadvantages: Taking the funds as income might mean paying high taxes on a larger amount. The money will no longer accumulate tax sheltered. If you are under 59½, you will pay a 10 percent federal tax penalty and perhaps a state tax penalty.

b. Leave the Money in the Plan if You Can

You can leave the money in the plan if permitted by the plan and the retirement plan laws (e.g., if you are age 70½, you may have to start taking distributions).

Advantages: Money will be managed the same way it has been in the past. No decisions need to be made as to where to invest your money. Money will be taxed as it is paid out.

Disadvantages: You cannot have direct control over your funds, or may not have as immediate access to the money as if it were in your own IRA account. Furthermore, once you start receiving annuity or installment payments, you cannot use the special income averaging or capital gains methods which apply only to lump sums.

c. Transfer Your Funds into a Rollover IRA

You can take an eligible rollover distribution from the plan and transfer the assets to an IRA.

Advantages: You can directly control where your money is invested and how the money is distributed to you. You are not taxed on amounts rolled to an IRA (within 60 days of the distribution) until they are distributed to you from the IRA.

Disadvantages: Not only must you choose the investment for your money, you must find one that will allow for and administer an IRA rollover. There may be a fee to invest and an ongoing administration cost.

Money distributed from an IRA is not eligible for forward income averaging or capital gains treatment that might be otherwise available.

Note that if you want to roll a distribution to an IRA, the best way to handle the transfer is by a "direct rollover" from the qualified plan's trustee to the IRA custodian. Otherwise, if the payout from the plan is made to the participant directly, the law requires that the plan withhold 20 percent of the distribution for income taxes. Then, the participant has 60 days to roll the funds to the IRA, and if the participant cannot come up with funds to replace the amount withheld by the plan, the 20 percent portion remains taxable.

D. Watch Out for the "Success" Taxes

You can take up to $155,000 (indexed for inflation) per year out of your retirement plans and pay the normal federal and state (if applicable) income taxes on the amount withdrawn. However, any distribution over $155,000 in any year is considered an "excess distribution" by the IRS and is subject to an additional tax of 15 percent on the amount over $155,000 Note: This extra tax has been suspended from January 1, 1997 through December 31, 1999.

An "excess accumulation" excise tax may also be required at the time of death. If the amount in all qualified retirement plans is more than the amount required to provide an income of $155,000 (as indexed for inflation) for the life expectancy of the participant, a 15 percent excise tax is levied on the excess of that total. For example, the estate of a 65-year-old participant, at the time of death, would be required to pay an excise tax on everything over approximately $1,100,000 (based on actuarial tables) from all of the individual's retirement plans. This excise tax has **not** been suspended from January 1, 1997, through December 31, 1999, for plans valued at time of death.

For people who have these higher amounts in retirement plans, evaluation should be done to determine when it might make sense to stop contributing to retirement plans and when to start taking the money out. Also, note that special rules apply to those employees who made a "grandfather election" under these excise tax rules.

ACTION: *If you are unsure of whether you will be able to retire, contact an RIA or Certified Financial Planner to run a retirement projection for you.*

If you are nearing retirement, contact an RIA, Certified Financial Planner, employee benefits attorney, or CPA to examine options for:

1. *Whether to roll over your retirement plan funds to an IRA or take the money and pay the taxes;*

2. *How you will structure your investments to get the income you need monthly to live; and*

3. *Compliance with all the rules. There are penalties for withdrawing too little or too much money and for withdrawing too early or too late.*

If you have over $1 million in retirement plan assets, you should have a distribution plan done that determines the best withdrawal plan considering your income needs and all related taxes—income taxes, excess distribution excise tax, excess accumulation excise tax, and estate taxes.

Conclusion

We hope our book has provided you, the business owner, with a basic understanding of how retirement plans work and what your responsibilities are in seeing that they provide future financial security for yourself and your employees.

As attorneys and registered investment advisors, we are often consulted after the plan(s) have been in existence for several years and problems have already arisen. We urge you to bring onto your team those professionals **from the very beginning** who will assure that you comply with the rules and protect plan assets so that you need not face disastrous consequences down the road. If plan assets are improperly invested or if a plan is disqualified because of noncompliance, the damage may never be undone. Thousands of dollars in future retirement income can be lost, as well as the possibility of the loss of thousands of dollars in penalties today.

We strongly encourage anyone with a retirement plan already in existence or thinking of setting one up in the future to consult with an employee benefits attorney, a registered investment advisor, and a qualified pension administrator to determine if they are currently in compliance and what steps need to be taken to assure that they remain in compliance throughout the life of the plan.

Authors' Biographies and Resumés

Jeffrey C. Chang—is a shareholder in the law firm of Chang, Ruthenberg & Long Law Corporation. Jeff specializes in profit sharing and pension plans, as well as various other deferred compensation and employee benefits matters. Jeff is the founder of the Sacramento Employee Benefits Roundtable, has taught deferred compensation and qualified retirement plans courses in the Master of Laws in Taxation program at McGeorge School of Law, and is a former member of the Executive Committee of the State Bar's Taxation Section. In 1990, Jeff founded the Employee Benefits Committee of the State Bar Tax Section and served as its chair during 1990 and 1991. Jeff currently serves on the IRS subcommittee of the American Society of Pension Actuaries (ASPA) Government Affairs Enforcement Committee. Jeff received a B.A. in Economics from U.C. Berkeley in 1976, and a J.D. from U.C. Davis School of Law in 1979.

Kenneth W. Ruthenberg, Jr.—is the managing shareholder of the Sacramento employee benefits law firm of Chang, Ruthenberg & Long Law Corporation. He has an extensive background in qualified retirement plans, nonqualified deferred compensation plans, and welfare benefit plans. Ken is a co-founder of the Employee Benefits Roundtable of Sacramento and is a past president of the organization. He is a graduate of the University of Kansas (B.S. 1969) and Hastings Collage of the Law (J.D. 1974), and earned his LL.M. (Tax) from Golden Gate University of Law (1985). Ken has also served as an adjunct professor of the McGeorge School of Law, where he taught the class on employee compensation in the Master of Laws in Taxation program, and as an adjunct professor of the Golden Gate University Graduate School of Taxation, where he taught the class on retirement plans in the Masters of Taxation program. He is a frequent speaker and author on the tax and legal aspects of employee benefits.

Elfrena Foord—is a principal in the financial services firm Foord, Van Bruggen & Ebersole Financial Services. She is a graduate of the University of Nevada (1966) in accounting. She received her CPA in 1969, her Certified Financial Planner designation in 1983, and is an Accredited Investment Management Consultant as of 1993. Elfrena served as the President of the Sacramento chapter of the international Association for Financial Planning, where she received the Chapter service award in 1991. She was recognized in 1987 by Money Magazine as one of the best financial planners nationwide. In 1992, she was honored as the YWCA's Outstanding Woman in Business.

Carol Van Bruggen—is a principal of the firm Foord, Van Bruggen & Ebersole Financial Services. She specializes in retirement plan investment consulting and has been involved in the financial industry since 1979. She holds the designation of Certified Financial Planner and Accredited Investment Management Consultant. She is a Registered Investment Advisor and past President of the International Association for Financial Planning, where she received the Chapter service award in 1992. She is the President of the Sacramento Chapter of the Western Pension & Benefits Conference and well known in her profession.

Chuck Ebersole—is a principal of the firm Foord, Van Bruggen & Ebersole Financial Services. He is a graduate of California State University of Sacramento with a B.S. degree in accounting. He received his Chartered Life Underwriter designation in 1980, his Chartered Financial Consultant designation in 1982, his Life Underwriter Training Council Fellow designation in 1984, and his Certified Financial Planner designation in 1995. He authored a book for LIMRA, titled *The Value of Beyond Expectation Service*. He works extensively in the areas of estate planning, social capital planning, and insurance planning. He is currently the secretary of the Sacramento Estate Planning Council. He also does extensive speaking and conducts educational seminars on financial, retirement, and social capital planning.

About Our Firms

Teamwork is a buzz word for the 1990s, but it's particularly important to use teamwork to have a retirement plan run smoothly. There are always at least three players in any retirement plan situation: the sponsor, the trustee, and the participants. In some situations, there may be up to seven or eight players. The proper selection and coordination of these players can make a huge difference in having a smooth-running plan versus a mess.

We, the authors, are two retirement plan specialty firms. We have extensive experience in working with retirement plans.

Chang, Ruthenberg & Long is a law firm that concentrates on the tax and non-tax aspects of employee benefit plans. Our services in the retirement plan area range from advising sponsors and fiduciaries on all aspects of qualified retirement plans (including design, documentation, set up, plan administration, reporting, fiduciary representation, and termination) and representing employers and trustees in employee benefit related IRS audits and tax controversies and DOL investigations, to obtaining determination letters, private letter rulings, DOL advisory opinions, and prohibited transaction exemptions for employers, fiduciaries, and participants.

Foord, Van Bruggen & Ebersole Financial Services is a financial planning and investment management firm that analyzes a company's retirement plan investment needs and recommends the investment strategies that are the most appropriate for effective growth of assets and ease of management for that particular company. As part of our services, we develop investment policy statements to assure compliance with ERISA requirements.

The strategic alliance of our two firms was born out of our experience of the many challenges that confront retirement plans when they are not well managed and coordinated. Our firms feel that problems do not need to happen. People, when educated and when they hire needed expertise, can prevent disasters. Companies can have an effective and smooth-running retirement plan that is a true financial benefit to both the employer and the employees alike.

Our firms work on a nationwide basis and are available for consultation.

Chang, Ruthenberg & Long Law Corporation
8880 Cal Center Drive, Suite 250
Sacramento, California 95826
(916) 362-5558
fax (916) 362-2825

Foord, Van Bruggen & Ebersole Financial Services
2255 Watt Avenue, Suite 300
Sacramento, California 95825
(916) 487-8700
fax (916) 487-4588

Index

T

Target Benefit Plans, 16

Tax Penalties, 69-70

Third-Party Administrator (TPA), 25

Third Party Trustee, 43

Top-Heavy Rules, 4

Trustees, 24, 43

U

UBTI (Unrelated Business Taxable Income), 27, 57, 58

V

Vesting, 4, 19, 23, 25, 61

Order Your Copies Today

Fax (916) 487-4588 or return this reply card.

QTY.	TITLE	PRICE	TOTAL
____	**Business Owner's Retirement Plan Survival Guide**	$19.95	_____
	CA residents please add applicable sales tax		_____
	Shipping/handling	$ 4.00	_____
	(add 50¢ for each additional book)		
	Grand Total		_____
	Call for quantity pricing when ordering 50 copies or more.		

☐ Check or money order enclosed with order
☐ Visa
☐ MasterCard
☐ American Express

Credit card acct. # _____

Exp. Date _____

Signature _____
(above required for all charges)

Ship book to:

Name _____

Organization _____

Address _____

City _____

State _____ Zip _____

Phone (   ) _____

Foord, Van Bruggen & Ebersole
2255 Watt Avenue, Suite 300
Sacramento, CA 95825-9598
(800) 494-7576

Notes

Notes

Notes

Notes